A TIME TO PLAY,

Reflections
on Childhood
and Creativity

MIRIAM HUFFMAN ROCKNESS

Zondervan Publishing House
of The Zondervan Corporation
Grand Rapids, Michigan

A TIME TO PLAY

© 1983 by Miriam Huffman Rockness

Library of Congress
Cataloging in Publication Data

Rockness, Miriam Huffman
   A time to play.

   Includes bibliographical references.
   1. Play. 2. Children.
3. Child psychology.
4. Creative ability in children.
5. Parenting.
I. Title.

HQ782.R62   1983   155.4'18   82-25096
ISBN 0-310-45871-4

Edited by
Linda Vanderzalm and Judith E. Markham
Designed by Kim Koning

The poem "Teddy Bear" from *Now We Are
Six* by A. A. Milne, copyright 1927 by
E. P. Dutton & Co., Inc., renewal 1955 by
A. A. Milne, reprinted by permission of
E. P. Dutton, Inc., McClelland and
Stewart, and Methuen.

Unless otherwise noted, Scripture is from
The New International Version, © 1978
by New York International Bible Society.

Printed in the United States of America

83   84   85   86   87   88 — 9   8   7   6   5   4   3   2   1

Lovingly,
to David, Kimberly, and Jonathan
who, with me, explore potentialities in themselves and the world.

CONTENTS

Acknowledgments   8

Introduction   9

Prologue
Signatures of Childhood   14
Free to Grow   18

The Encouragers
"How Does Your Garden Grow?"   24
Daddy's Home!   27
Fanning the Fire   30
The Stage Is Set   32
The Education of Kimberly   34
The Cost of Creativity   38
Collection Obsession   40
Who's Raising Our Children?   43

Fit for a Child
More Than a House   46
The Security of Being Sure   48
Mission Impossible   50
Shadowed   54
Making a Mess   57
"It's Not Fair"   60
Traditions   62
Time To Be Alone   65
A Lament   68
Secrets   72

Stocking the Child's Workshop
The Work of a Child Is Play   76
Let's Pretend!   79
Affairs of the Heart   82
No Trespassing!   86
Signature of Man   89
Games Children Play   94

The Broadening World
Breaking Mind Barriers   98
First Try Policy   100
The Scent of Fear   103
Rite of Reading   106
The Rarest Kind of Best   110
Nights at the Round Table   113
Budgeting an Adventure   115
Adventure Without a Pricetag   117
How Wide Is Our World?   120

A Way of Seeing

The Creative Process   124
Limitations   126
Eyes That See   129
A Sense of Wonder   132
Making of a Mind   136

A Child's Worth

The Measure of Worth   140
Failure   144
Conformity and Self-Acceptance   146
Cat Got Your Tongue?   150
All by Myself   154
Blue Ribbon for Kimberly   157
A Listening Heart   159
And Things That Go Bump in the Night   162
Facing Fences   166
The Goal   169
Loved—No Matter What!   171

All They Are Meant To Be

The Source   174
Save Me From Myself!   176
Teach Thy Children   179
Too Busy to Train   182
To Spank or Not to Spank   185
What Do Our Children Need?   188
Beyond Behavior   190
Broken Pieces   193
The Way   197

Epilogue   201

Notes   203

Recommended Reading   204

ACKNOWLEDGMENTS

Many people "write" the book which is finally published under one name: families who shape a life; books and thoughts of individuals who influence thinking; friends who stand by with aid, suggestions, and encouragement. *A Time To Play* is no exception. To my unnamed collaborators—thank you!

Special acknowledgments go to my husband, Dave, who made this book possible through his belief in me, his active support in the writing process, and his extraordinary involvement in the family; to Milford Myhre, who through relentlessly exacting and perceptive chapter-by-chapter editing taught me more than I thought necessary about the English language; and to Anne Stovall, who spent countless hours deciphering and typing the original manuscript.

INTRODUCTION

This is a book about childhood. My first book, *Keep These Things*, reflected my transition from being my mother's daughter to becoming my children's mother. Here the focus shifts from myself to my children. I continue to struggle with conflicts between my own desires and the needs of my children. Nevertheless I have come to terms with preserving my identity as a woman while fulfilling the role of mother. More urgent to me now is the emerging identity of each of my three children, whose rapid developments signal poignant reminders that they are growing up to go away. The influence which their father and I have on their lives is thus limited to a relatively brief span of time.

As my responsibilities gradually transfer from the physical care of young children to the more subtle yet vitally important needs of their developing personalities, I ask myself fundamental questions about preparing them for future life. How do I nurture that which is unique in my children? How do I respect each one's individuality while also respecting the family as a whole? What kind of home environment is the most conducive to nurturing the creative instinct in my children? What additional experiences should I be providing for them? What helps young people develop a confidence that is sufficiently strong to sustain rigorous self-evaluation and the comparisons to others? How may I help them to bolster those traits of character which will assist their abilities to attain full bloom? In short, *how do I help them realize their full potential?*

Such questions have led me to read about and reflect on the nature of creativity and the lives of creative people. I have found that there are certain factors which universally encourage creative expression: the support and encouragement of sensitive people; an environment conducive to creative experimentation; availability of materials and tools to express creative inclinations; exposure to a wide variety of people, places, and experiences. I have discovered that creative people have developed a perspective, a way of seeing that is in itself creative. Furthermore, creative people need to develop inner qualities of confidence and strength of character in order to weather the storms inherent in creative work.

Ironically while contemporary American culture seems to place a high premium on creativity, much offered to children in its name actually jeopardizes creativity. Society applauds innovations, change, and freedom of expression. True creativity, however, lies not in the rejection of tradition or in keeping up with the times, or in expressing oneself without limits. Nor can creativity be scheduled into a particular time slot or be administered by specific organizations. Creativity goes beyond any given work, novelty, or change. It is a way of seeing, or ordering the raw materials of choice and circumstance. It is a way of *being*.

My observations, though perhaps disturbing to a society which is prone to offer superficial solutions to profound problems, may have heartening implications for the family. Parents, I'm convinced, are in the best possible position to provide conditions most conducive to creativity; the home provides the best possible environment.

This book is my attempt to think through and apply my understandings of childhood and creativity in the context of everyday living. It is not a "how to" book, but rather it offers some "thinking out loud" about passionate concerns regarding my children's development: shyness, fear, sibling jealousy, the effects of criticism, the conflict between my creative needs and those of my children, the role of the school vs. that of the home, my children's "failure," the selection of tools to implement my children's creative urgings, working within financial and geographic limitations, dealing with my children's resistance to new ideas, fostering a creative approach to daily situations, providing discipline without stifling my children's spirits, parental mistakes—to name but some. While wrestling with the complexities of daily situations, I am faced over and over again with a simple reality: this is my situation; what am I going to do about it?

In seeking out possible solutions, I am thankful that I am not without lamps to point the way. I consult "experts," seeking the council of those who have walked the path before me. I compare notes with other mothers. I lean on the wisdom and strength of my husband. I check my thinking against scriptural principles. Then I proceed cautiously, pleading guidance from my heavenly Father. For a mother, as for others, learning is doing, doing is learning.

This is a book about childhood. The dominant theme is creativity in its fullest sense: potentiality. I hope that by sharing my experiences, I will encourage others to help their children become all they were meant to be.

The Child is father of the Man.
William Wordsworth

PROLOGUE

To be a child is to see with the eyes of a child—it is a way of seeing.

SIGNATURES OF CHILDHOOD

Childhood is the morning time of creativity. Children are receptive to all of the wonders of the world spread before them. To children, everything is new and fresh and glowing.

Childhood is a special, one-and-only time in life. It is marked by characteristics so unique to those particular years that they could be called *signatures of childhood*. These signatures, I believe, give childhood its memorable character.

A sense of wonder. Children have an innate openness to the world; they are captivated by both the cosmic majesty of changing seasons and the intricate weaving of a spider's web. The universe is a treasure chest filled with bounty; children's senses are the keys to unlock it. Their inborn curiosity is continually fanned by the inexhaustible cache before them. Unhampered by the rigid time frame of the adult, children are at liberty to probe and savor. They follow a ladybug, mesmerized by her shiny red hood, determined to pursue her to the earth's edge. With unerring ear they detect music in the still night air: "I like the song nighttime sings—'cheep, cheep, cheep!'" They delight in inchworms methodically measuring off their length, in fireflies illuminating the darkness with flickering torches, in icicles dropping dazzling diamonds from spears of crystal. Children simply delight! Can one ever completely forget the rush of joy on hearing the music-box tune of the ice cream truck, the awe in awakening one morning to find the earth swathed in the stark white of freshly fallen snow? With sensibilities undulled and unjaded, children respond to both the microscopic and the monumental with joy, surprise, and wonder!

Spirit of high adventure. With an insatiable curiosity and a bent for discovery, the child is a natural explorer. Before the child lies the entire world, untraveled, unexplored. Is the leap over a wall into unknown territory any less a conquest for a child than was the Pacific Ocean for Balboa or America for Columbus? Each leap expands the child's view, whetting the appetite for the next adventure. Some children are more daring than others, but all, within the reach of their courage, are indeed explorers. In attic or pond, basement or jungle, the spirit is the same.

> Tell him Earth
> That he has deed and title
> To beauty by the acre
> Anywhere he breathes.
>
> *Frances Frost*

Children's spirits of adventure are heightened by a *fertile imagination* fed with hopes and dreams, bouyed by a future of possibilities. Like sponges their minds soak up images of the world and wring out tales and fancies. Children are forever testing out roles, trying one, discarding it for another. "What shall I be?" is a heady question for one who can be *anything!* Their vocational choice is determined by the most recent input; yesterday a fireman, today a baseball player; at one moment a teacher, at the next an artist. With the magic wand of fancy, a bunk bed might be transformed into a fire engine, a clump of overgrowth into a jungle fort, a bathtub into an ocean, a sidewalk into "dry land," and surrounding grass into quicksand! The other day three-year-old Jonathan announced, "I went to the circus yesterday."

"Who took you?" I questioned.

"I went all by myself," he boasted.

"You did?" I exclaimed in mock surprise.

"I walked down the steps, past our lawn, past the flag, and down the walk to the sidewalk with the white house. And there was a circus!"

"What did you see?" I asked.

"A tiger and a donkey and a elephant and a lion and a, and a . . . and two clowns!"

Components of mundane, everyday experience are adapted, modified, combined, and reshaped into fantasies of their own.

Paradoxically, despite children's preoccupation with the distant future, childhood is marked by an *intense living in the present*. Children live fully the all-encompassing *now*, throbbing, pulsating with the immediacy of childhood. To them "a mere twenty-four hours of future time resembles an impermeable sheet of plate glass."[1] Nothing matters except today. Children are hardly interested in the long-range benefits of doing finger exercises or of brushing one's teeth or of learning good table manners. In the timelessness of the eternal present is an urgent immediacy. Sorrows are sharper, but at the same time they are of shorter duration. A child's world comes to a grinding halt by a spanking, a plate full of peas, or exclusion from a privileged group. Five minutes later the spanked child emerges wreathed in smiles, emanating goodwill; peas are forgotten in dessert; rejection is eased by a new alliance. The excruciating dread of a shot is erased by the glory of a new bandage. Miseries are more intense, but likewise are the joys. Just as children are swallowed whole by their sorrows, they are totally transported by their ecstacy!

Perhaps one of the loveliest signatures of childhood, from an adult point of view, is *freedom from ultimate responsibility*. "Children are guests at this feast and are not responsible for what is on the table."[2] Somehow, from somewhere, three proper meals are set before them daily; clothes the right size (give or take an inch or two) hang in their closets; decisions are made regarding their education. Someone fusses over and attends to their colds and aches and pains. While children may chafe over the choices and decisions made on their behalf, such is the luxury of security. Children may rail against having to make a bed, set a table, or sweep a walk, but these responsibilities are minimal in comparison to the responsibilities of providing that bed, supplying food for that table, or putting a roof over the house at the end of that freshly swept walk. How many times has a disappointed, "My parents say I can't," been mixed with reluctant relief? What adults, at some time or other, wouldn't gladly exchange their authority for freedom from ultimate responsibility?

The final signature of childhood is *change*. The first years of any child's life are marked by considerable changes in size, physical appearance, emotional controls, and mental ability, to name a few. Along with these changes inevitably come growing pains, but despite the pain, there is much that is positive about growth and change. With growth comes the satisfaction of mastering new skills: skipping, tying shoelaces, coloring within the lines, reading books, telling time, and playing the piano. With change in children's bodies comes the exhilaration of increased power and control: feeding oneself, walking for the first time, reaching the counter without needing a stool, catching a baseball, and riding a bicycle. Children expend a great deal of energy adjusting to changes in their lives. Sometimes when they are overwhelmed by the unrelenting progressive movement, they cling to the familiar. The same son who yesterday begged for more privileges lapses today into baby talk. Once children have embarked on the perilous journey of life, the direction is irreversible: forward, march!

Signatures of childhood: a sense of wonder, the spirit of high adventure, a fertile imagination, living in the present, freedom from ultimate responsibility, and change. These, of course, do not add up to perfection. Bittersweet are they! Yet surely in these signatures are essences worth cherishing for all time—not mere sentiments but essences from which sturdy futures are built.

FREE TO GROW

There is a time for everything,
and a season for every activity
under heaven.

Ecclesiastes 3:1

Childhood is a foundational time. It is a time to build habits, a time to mold characters, a time to shape personalities. James Russell Lowell advises us to "build sure in the beginning." Roots grow slowly, but given time to penetrate deeply into the earth, they provide strong, firm, lifetime support.

Childhood is also a time for the exploration and experimentation which lead children to the discovery of the physical world, of themselves, and of their place in the scheme of things. Childhood is a time to taste and touch, to meander and probe. By capitalizing on these aspects of childhood which are favorable to creativity, we school our children in a way of seeing. With the aid of loving, sensitive adults children learn to imaginatively shape the raw materials of life. They learn to become artists in living.

On the surface it appears that our children are free to grow, free to develop their potential. Their childhood has not been marked by malnutrition or physical abuse. Their early years have not been spent in hard labor in factories or in fields. Their childhood years have not been scarred by war and its devastation. We live in a country and a time that smiles on its young. In this century and in this decade there are many supports for our children: legislation on their behalf, emphasis on quality education, and the many parental aids to child rearing.

Despite all of this focus on the child, there exist in our society undercurrents which are hostile to childhood. In order for our children to be truly free to grow, in order for our children to experience childhood in the fullest and richest sense, we parents must not only be aware of these hostile undercurrents, but we must also be willing to aggressively combat them.

One of the threats to our children's experience is that our society has become experience-greedy. As Americans, our basic needs have been

18

amply met. We abound in time and resources to pursue luxuries. Airline advertisements beckon us to "Experience the Orient." Friends encourage us to experience a new sport or experience a new restaurant. In response to this we often feel overwhelmed by "experience-overload." This same overload has filtered into our children's lives. We feel duty bound to compress in the daily allotment of twenty-four hours all manner of good experiences for our children. Backing one experience against the other, we leave little time for the child to pause, to wonder. This trend is compounded by an emphasis on achievement. Children are pushed prematurely into specializations and highly competitive situations. All of the glorious "results" blind us from the reality: the loss of a freewheeling, open-ended exploration stage which is so essential to self-discovery. Television competes vigorously for the little remaining time, transforming the child into a mute spectator whose imagination is numbed by endless images and details. The signatures of childhood include a spirit of high adventure, a sense of wonder, a fertile imagination. When can today's children leisurely explore? When can they linger to touch and taste and savor? When can they spin dreams and schemes?

Another threat to the childhood experience is the role uncertainty felt by parents. Our culture has placed a value on youth that borders on child-worship. Parents are confused by conflicting advice from the experts. They are intimidated by a view of the child as a miniature adult and are uncertain of their role in relation to their child. Little wonder that parents permit "family functions" to be usurped by outside organizations. Little wonder that parents abdicate their right to authority altogether. But what is the effect? In the absence of parental involvement, children are shaped by schools, the media, and their peer groups. However important a role these play as supplements in a child's development, they are not adequate replacements for consistent parental nurture. The lack of parental authority deprives the child of needed direction, guidance, and security.

A third threat to childhood lies in the fact that our society discourages the self-sacrifice which is essential to high quality parenting. Ours is a "me first" generation. We are told to meet our own needs first; we are told that our personal "rights" take priority over the rights and needs of others. This mentality hardly prepares parents for the exhausting demands of raising children. In every other vocation, rigorous training and personal sacrifice are assumed as prerequisites to quality performance. Why should parenthood be different? At the heart of parenthood is a constant tension between personal needs and the needs of one's children. This essentially human conflict between rights and self-giving is further complicated for today's woman by the numerous alternatives available to her. Tantalized by colorful career options on the one hand and faced with dreary certainties of mothering on the other hand, a woman needs sound judgment and far-sightedness which is uncharacteristic of today's young. And there remains that haunting question, "So what?" So I pour out my "best years" for my children, so I put aside my hard won training and skills for the present time, what assurances have I that my children will "turn out" well? There are all too many indications that I could give and give and give—to no avail. Why not take care of the one person over whom I *do* have control? Myself. Why not? To provide children with a quality childhood exacts a high personal price from parents. Is it worth the price?

I gain comfort in reviewing specific measures my husband and I have taken to structure a lifestyle supportive to the family; I find consolation in considering decisions we have made in the best interest of our children. And yet I know only too well how easily I slip into the very patterns of thinking and living we so boldly disclaim. All too frequently I become caught up in a frenzy of activities, pulling the children with me. Too many times the children's choices rule the day because of my indecisiveness or inaccessibility. Far too often the *children* lose in that battle continuously waging within me: my desires vs. their needs.

These negative trends in our society insidiously and subtly creep into our lives and threaten to rob our children of a full childhood experience. We parents must recognize these threats and must be willing to safeguard our children's experience by combating these trends in our own lives.

It is my overwhelming desire to give my children the gift of a rich childhood. You perhaps share that goal with me. Giving this gift demands more of us than sentiment or good intentions. It demands a conscious effort on our part to provide an environment that allows our children to reach their full created potential. To this end:

1. We parents must assume the role of "encouragers," supporting our children in the discovery and development of their innate gifts and abilities.

2. We parents must structure a home environment which is conducive to the nurture and enrichment of our children.

3. We parents must provide "tools" for a wide range of exploration and experimentation, knowing that in the hands of our children these tools will not only chisel their dreams and schemes but will also test their potentialities.

4. We parents must expose our children to a wide variety of people, places, and experiences as an initiation to the rich possibilities of life.

5. We parents must foster an open, adventurous approach to daily living, understanding that true creativity is the "eyes" through which we see all of life.

6. We parents must build in our children the strong ego and indomitable spirit which is foundational to confident, creative expression.

7. We parents must offer our children moral and spiritual direction in the belief that true creativity is not the result of a free, unbridled spirit but of the creature in right relationship with the Creator.

THE ENCOURAGERS

Parents need to assume the role of encouragers, supporting their children in the discovery and development of their innate gifts and abilities.

"HOW DOES YOUR GARDEN GROW?"

"Rich man, poor man, beggar-man, thief; Doctor, lawyer, Indian chief." Whap—whap—whap—the jump rope whistles through the air, sharply slapping the hard concrete. Kimberly controls the rope with a deft twist of the wrist, rhythmically repeating her hop-skip pattern.

"One, two, three, four, five," children chant in chorus. "Six, seven, eight, nine, ten." Faster, faster, faster Kimberly jumps until, tangled in the rope, she trips to a breathless stop.

Children sing the songs and play the games of childhood. They faithfully observe rites and rules of play. What promises and possibilities are locked within children intent upon their games? What clues and hints are revealed through their play?

Take six-year-old Kimberly, for instance. Her grace and agility belie the physical stamina required for this activity of endurance. She is a fine-boned, delicate child who favored, we thought, the stereotyped "little girl" activities—dolls, playing house, and coloring books. Her athletic development has recently emerged and has taken us mildly by surprise. We wonder what other surprises are hidden within her.

David, Jonathan, and Kimberly—three children with gifts and capabilities yet unknown. What secrets lie buried deep within these complex, individual persons? How do we parents, entrusted with the care and keeping of young children, help them achieve their true potential? Where do we begin?

I hold in my hand an open packet of mixed seeds: shiny black dots, dull tan splinters, dark burr-like rounds—a collection of countless shapes, colors, and textures. The small, dry contents of the package do not bear the slightest resemblance to the dazzling display of flowers promised on the envelope's cover. Nonetheless I am assured that by faithfully following the directions printed on the packet, the seeds will blossom into the glorious reds, pinks, yellows, blues, whites, and golds pictured on the envelope. I select a bristly, semicircle of brown. What will it become? A primrose? A daisy? A mum? There is nothing on the surface that suggests its design. All that I can do is provide the proper conditions for growth—nourishing soil, sun, water. Then I must stand back and wait. The secret is in the seed.

As the secret of the flower is in the seed, so the secret of each child is within the individual. We parents are gardeners; our children are the seeds. We do not know the design locked within each child, but we do know what we must do. Whether the flower is marigold, aster, larkspur, or rose, the instructions read the same: "Plant in good garden soil in a sunny area. Keep evenly moist." We must cultivate the seedbed and provide proper nourishment for the seed. Then we must stand back and wait.

Like the developing seedlings, children soon show hints and indications of their inner design. Our parental care must then become ever more specialized and suited to each particular growing individual. We must search for the union between the child's inner desires and the outward expressions. As caretakers, we parents are in the best possible position to provide optimal conditions to help our children attain full bloom.

Of course growth is not quite this simple either with children or with plants! Warnings on seed packets suggest precautions: "Use care to avoid covering fine seed too deeply or leaving larger seeds exposed at surfaces. Some seeds germinate faster than others so allow time for slower sprouts to emerge." The process from seed to sprout to full bloom is threatened by blight and bruising.

It seems so clear with a handful of seeds. There is nothing in the world I can do to produce an aster from a petunia seed. I can hope for an aster or even pray for an aster, but a petunia seed will always produce a petunia. If I have not accepted the essence of the seed, I can only be frustrated by the flower. If I'm hoping for an aster, a petunia can only be a disappointment. However, a petunia—free to fully be a petunia—can be a source of pleasure and delight.

So it is with children. The directions are clear as are the warnings. I must tend and nourish the children entrusted to my care. I must be watching, listening, ever sensitive to hints and indications of their inner design. I must always be ready to aid and assist with their dreams and schemes. Likewise, I must stand back, humble before their intuition, and let them blossom in their own time and in their own way. "This is how the flowers grow, I have watched them and I know."[3]

TO A SMALL CHILD

In the eyes of the world
You are the merest shell,
A hull or pod
Waiting to be filled.
But in the eyes of God, yes, God,
You are the very self
He willed.
And yet, you are very self,
Contained.

Darcy Heath

DADDY'S HOME!

"Mommy, may I water the flowers?" Jonathan asks.

"Not now, Jonathan. I have to hose down the porch—and it's too close to suppertime anyway."

"Well, may I take off my shoes and play in the water?" he persists.

"If you promise not to get your clothes wet."

"Hurrah!" Jonathan throws his shoes on the grass, then carefully rolls the legs of his pants to his knees.

"Kimberly! We may play in the water!" he announces to his sister, who suddenly appears on the front lawn.

Together they play, following tiny tributaries of water down the sidewalk to where the streams flow into one grand river. I spray baskets of hanging plants; the children shriek with delight when the breeze hits them with a mist of water.

A familiar white car rounds the corner and slowly edges up to the curb. "Daddy's home! Daddy's home!" the children shout in joyful chorus. Without so much as a backwards glance, they desert their water play to run alongside the moving vehicle. When it comes to a stop, they open the door and all but pull their father from the car.

David appears from the backyard, bat and ball in hand. "Hey, dad! Pitch me a ball!" He wings a tennis ball at his father who quickly disengages himself from the two little beings hanging on his arms.

"Let's all play ball," he sagely suggests. While they improvise an impromptu game of baseball, I return to the kitchen to put hamburgers in the skillet.

"Daddy's home!" What an effect that cry of joy has on our young! Play is abandoned; pain is forgotten—all for the pleasure brought by his presence!

I am grateful for Dave's strong presence in our family. I am always relieved that there are two of us who share the responsibilities of shaping our children's lives. There are areas of parenting that Dave handles with greater strength and wisdom than I could. There are special qualities of character which only he can model for our children. He has a unique way of stirring up within our children interests and abilities that might other-wise be hidden. He holds great influence in their lives.

Daddy's assistance in a homework assignment invariably enhances the project, be it research on a president of the United States, the perusal of old newspapers to locate a graph, or a trip to the dime store to purchase needed materials. How proud the children are as he examines the results of their efforts—the laboriously formed letters of the alphabet, the columns of painstakingly computed numbers, the poem copied into a hand-bound book. Proximity demands that I maintain piano practice routines, but when Dave sits down to accompany a child in a duet or sits back to enjoy a solo performance, motivation reaches new heights. By including the children in his interests, he opens for them areas otherwise unexplored—a morning at the golf course, a late afternoon trip to the tennis court, an evening at the high school football game. The children even learn with Dave the demanding arias of his bass solos for Handel's *Messiah!* Through active involvement and appreciation, Dave helps the children discover and develop their gifts and abilities.

His very masculinity, to start with, has an obvious influence on the children. The boys unconsciously model their father's mannerisms, mimicking his gait, catching his expressions in their faces and speech. Kimberly, with unabashed adoration, basks in his bigness. His resonant voice imparts authority and produces results that I could not hope to achieve by voice alone.

He offers, as well, qualities that go beyond a male presence and a resounding voice. His insight frequently sheds light on situations that allude me. "The boys are teaming up against Kimberly, you know." Or, "I believe David needs more time apart from the younger children." Often when I hesitate before a door which, when opened, will lead the children to greater independence, he wisely turns the knob and gives the door a push: "I don't see why David can't ride his bike downtown." Or, "OK, Jonathan, you can go with David and Kimberly to visit Rocky. Just be sure to hold their hands when you cross the streets."

With fatherly understanding he sees the importance of baseball cleats and an aluminum bat for an aspiring Little Leaguer; he jumps to the defense of activities which seem to me to swallow unreasonable amounts of time: "It's good for her; she needs the time with other children." Or, "It's only for a few months; let him join." With matchless patience he approaches disciplinary problems that have long since exhausted me; he responds judiciously to situations which elicit only an emotional response from me.

Perhaps the children are unaware of the specific qualities which constitute their father's character. They are, however, fully aware of an element of adventure which he brings into their lives! "Daddies are more playful than mommies," Kimberly carefully observes. It is daddy who rounds up the family on Saturday for an unplanned trip to the zoo; it is daddy who stops everything to learn how to play the game of Uno. The finest literary works of A. A. Milne or Beatrix Potter cannot compare in the children's estimation to their father's own Squirrel Stories, whose characters bear a striking resemblance to the Rockness family and their friends.

I go to the kitchen door to call the baseball players in for supper. Daddy steps up to bat: "Get ready! I'm going to hit this ball over the fence." David pitches. Strike one. Strike two. Strike three. . . And he's out! The children hoot with laughter. He does, indeed, exhibit patience and perspective that elude me.

Yes, Dave offers special gifts to our children. And so do I. I provide routine, structure, and an overall "game plan" that serves as an invaluable complement to his contributions. I offer certain qualities unique to my personality. My appearance on the doorstep may not bring the ecstatic cry *Mommy's* home!" but there are indications along the way that my endeavors are appreciated. I suppose one could quibble about some inequities that work to his advantage with the children, but what's the point? What he provides for them—be it patience or perspective or whatever—not only enriches their lives but is a welcome support for me. Ours is a true collaboration: These are *our* children; we *both* contribute to their lives. What we give to them are gifts to each other. The proclamation "Daddy's home!" sends spirits soaring—and none, I avow, higher than mine!

FANNING THE FIRE

David huddles over a pile of pennies, carefully checking the date on each coin. The contents of his coin collecting kit are spread all over the dining room table. Occasionally this nine-year-old pulls out a magnifying glass and scrutinizes a particular coin or pages through a book, scanning down the narrow columns.

What holds him to the task at hand? Is it the possibility of finding a rare and valuable piece of currency? Is it the thrill of acquisition, penny by penny, nickel by nickel? Could it be the satisfaction of systematically filling in the dated coin holders with the correct coins, of completing a collection? Or is it the total fascination of all of these?

David's life changed significantly since his assistant principal brought a coin collection to David's classroom. He raids our piggy banks and daily picks our pockets, sifting through our loose change. The purchase of a "Beginner's Coin Collecting Kit" permitted his interest to sharpen and take a more sophisticated turn. Fortified with magnifying glass, coin folders, and handbooks, his search became intense and specific. He has ordered his entire family to be on the alert for "coins that are old or foreign or have the letter S."

David's father and I are admitted accomplices to his obsession: we bought the kit that fanned his fascination into full flame. A child's interest, we've long since discovered, is a matchless natural resource. When properly channeled and directed, a child's interest can accomplish feats beyond the capacity of sheer willpower. Consider that David, who rarely reads for the pure joy of reading, has spent countless hours devouring the printed page, attacking vocabulary words that are years beyond his age. Consider the historical data he has assimilated in his quest to identify certain coins. Consider the proficiency he has gained in mathematics as he computes complicated coin exchanges. Over and over the pattern repeats itself: A parent may plot or plead to involve a child in a task or an activity, but when a parent gives support to a child's interest, a mere spark of interest can then blaze into a roaring flame.

The opposite is also true. When a child's interest is neglected, that interest can smolder and sputter and be extinguished altogether. This summer, while vacationing by the ocean, the children quite naturally began to collect shells. Diligently they cleaned, sorted, and identified their findings. Once we were home, the younger children soon forgot about their collections. However, David's enthusiasm was rekindled when he saw his piano teacher's shell collection that was neatly labeled and stored in the tiny drawers of fishing tackle boxes. David pleaded with me daily to get him a display box for his shells; I procrastinated and put him off. When my actions finally caught up with my intentions, David restrained me with a halting, "Don't bother, mom, I'm really not so interested anymore." Failure to respond to his momentary interest by following up with necessary materials resulted in a lost opportunity.

David's coin collecting may never lead to a career in numismatics or any other currency-related science. With or without my encouragement David will most likely not choose oceanography as his life's work as the result of his shell collecting. However, much is to be gained from supporting a child's interest or passing fancy. Such experiences are part of the testing process which leads to a life's vocation or lifelong avocations. A child's interest is a parent's ally. Wise are the parents who recognize a spark of interest and add kindling to the fire!

THE STAGE IS SET

A veritable hum of activity permeates our mountain retreat as five children prepare for "Family Night," the annual talent night which our family shares with our friends, the Guests. This evening, after daddies return home and all children are ready for bed, our two families will gather in the living room for an "all-stops-out" variety show.

Tonight's program will include group singing, vocal ensembles, recorder solos, and rounds. Even three-year-old Jonathan figures inportantly in the evening's entertainment. He and Dave have spent many concentrated moments rehearsing a ventriloquist act. Jonathan will sit on Dave's lap and woodenly mouth the script while Dave pulls his invisible strings. Each year the preparations become increasingly elaborate; this year intricate choreography has been added using dramatic entrances and exits. A highlight of the night is the mountain song which we will all sing while marching to a brisk beat, and if that is not enough to test our coordination, the song breaks into a two-part yodel at the refrain. For the grand finale everyone will line up for the "hokey-pokey," much to the irrepressible delight of the children who watch their parents become totally uninhibited!

The children, buoyed by success of previous years' performances and spurred by anticipation, are lifted to unprecedented heights of creative activity. The discipline and dedication demonstrated throughout their preparations exceed anything we parents could elicit. The four older children line up on the sofa while they tediously drill recorder fingerings. David coaches the girls, and everyone experiments with possible special effects. Carrie Anne and Chelsea teach the Rockness children the words and gestures of a song. Presently Chelsea enlists Kimberly in assisting her in the crafting of puppets from paper bags—an additional dash of drama. Jonathan, uncharacteristically accommodating, gravitates from project to project to "help," when tolerated, or simply to observe.

Watching these industrious children, I cannot help but note the invaluable role that encouragement plays in the creative process. Clearly the reward of today's efforts will be tonight's sure hit before a full house. However much more is at work to produce such industry: the stimulation of exchanging ideas; the support and encouragement of the group when interest begins to flag; a relaxed atmosphere in which to work together or independently; the ready assistance in new challenges; the obvious acceptance by peers; the freedom to perform without competition.

Spontaneous, productive hours like these are rare, and they are impossible to structure or recapture. There are, however, notes to be taken and lessons to be learned from this excellent atmosphere for encouragement. True encouragement involves far more than easy praise or insincere compliments. It involves the ability to signal genuine interest; the perception to sense when assistance is needed and when it is not; the self-control to observe and listen without criticism or correction; the willingness to provide materials or instruction to implement a task. In a warm, accepting atmosphere the stage is set, and creativity begins to flow.

THE EDUCATION OF KIMBERLY

It is Kimberly's first full day of school. I watch as the car door slams shut and she begins her walk alone down that long sidewalk to the playground. She proceeds steadily, looking straight ahead, her ponytails bouncing jauntily with each step. She stops hesitantly at the edge of the playground. She looks so vulnerable standing in the distance, a spot of green in her little smocked jumper. Suddenly she breaks into a full run toward another girl who runs toward her. (Blessings on that child, whoever she is!) Together they disappear into a crowd of tiny people.

For one wrenching moment I stare at the brick building that will hold my child captive six hours each day for the next several years of her life. What effect will school have on this sprightly child? She reaches out so spontaneously to greet her world. From her mouth comes poetry; with chalk and paints she fills sidewalks and paper with color and line which are both rich and expressive. One moment she dances in lithe response to the rhythm and mood of her private world; the next moment she assumes a characterization with the flair of a Shakespearean actress.

Swallowed into the belly of public education, will she be fed only facts, leaving her imagination undernourished? Will she memorize formulas for thinking without exercising open-mindedness? Within the halls of learning will she trade in her sword of creativity for the armor of convention? Years later will she be spewed forth with millions of other children—a mere mechanical robot?

As my fears volley with my suspicions, new questions arise about the educational system. What do I expect from school? What should I expect? Should I expect a school to take large groups of children between the ages of six and eighteen each with diverse interests and abilities, and by holding class for a few hours a day produce an educated person or a creative person? On the other hand should I blame the schools for possible shortcomings in a child's development? Are my fears too great because my expectations are too high?

34

Jacques Barzun in *Teacher in America* insists that, "education is not merely schooling. It is a lifelong discipline of the individual." This process of education begins at birth, broadens as the toddler's world expands, is formalized the first day of school, and continues throughout life. Schooling is the teaching of knowledge considered useful to humanity; education, on the other hand, not only includes schooling but also embraces all other learning acquired through the sheer stimulation of being alive.

Who, then, is responsible for the child's education? Is the teacher who sees thirty children for six hours a day, five days a week, for nine months of one year? Or is education the responsibility of the parent who loves the child and who sees the child develop through the continuum of many years? To teachers, I believe, belongs the task of schooling, which, although a significant part of the educational process, is not in itself an education. To parents, then, falls the far greater task of educating the child, of exposing the child to the limitless experiences that will produce growth and learning.

Certainly the schools can be a great help in developing our children's abilities. Undoubtedly sensitive teachers will unearth hidden gifts in our children, but we cannot depend totally on the schools to do that job. It is ultimately the responsibility of the parents to help their children reach their full potential. Parents must always be ready to go beyond, to supplement the work of the schools.

When I assume the awesome role of educational overseer, I begin to view the school in an entirely different light. No longer does it loom as a monumental threat to my child's mind; rather I see the school as a bastion of knowledge that will greatly aid me in my task of educating three children.

Not for a moment do I minimize the responsibility of the schools. They are equipped for tasks which I am unqualified to perform. They hold in their keeping the keys to unlock doors in the endless corridors of learning; for many children the schools provide the only formal exposure to knowledge. Indeed they have a great responsibility: one of my responsibilities is to remind them of this.

Nevertheless I am enough of a realist to know that mass education, like mass *anything*, has built-in limitations, limitations that are compounded by human fallibility. In the total sweep of schooling there will be good years and bad years. Some teachers will be strong in certain areas but weak in others. I trust that the good years will balance out the bad ones.

However when significant gaps appear in my children's schooling, those gaps become *my* problem. If I don't assume this responsibility for filling gaps in their education, who will? I can approach the teacher with my concern, but if there is no response, I must be prepared to compensate accordingly. If I grumble for an entire school year because there is no art in Kimberly's room, but do not have it within me to purchase a tin of paints or a tub of clay to accommodate her need for a creative outlet, then I, too, have fallen short. If I am aware of weaknesses in a child's reading program or math or geography, there is nothing to stop me from going to the library or from making math flash cards or from purchasing a globe. Who knows what wonders can be wrought with a teacher-pupil ratio of one to three? I grant that there are others who are more qualified than I, but surely at the grade-school level I can devise games and gimmicks to augment my child's learning. If I do not care enough at least to try, I simply do not care enough!

Always I must keep in mind the larger picture. I must remember that instruction from any source is but one aspect of the learning process. Education is much broader than spelling lists, math formulas, or word drills. Greater wisdom and more profound knowledge will be acquired through self-teaching, however richly the process is aided by teacher grit or parent wit.

What will kindle that spark of interest in a child's mind and set it ablaze for learning? Perhaps it will be the encouragement and rapport of a teacher and student; maybe it will be an experience which I have carefully planned. It may as likely be an insight or revelation from play or from a child's peers.

Parents and teachers can furnish a child's mind with a wealth of knowledge; we can prod and provoke the thought processes, but ultimately we must humbly stand back and wait for the chance perception that will break over the child like morning light, illuminating the pathway to a lifetime of learning.

I see Kimberly again, a wee figure in green, on the ladder of a steep slide. Up, up, up, she climbs. At the top she sits and pleats the folds of her skirt around her. Down, down, down—swish—she lands with a flying jump upon her feet. Yes, whether it be slide or desk, playground or classroom, home, school, church, club—they're all of one piece. All collaborate in the process that has been going on for six years and will continue throughout her life: the education of Kimberly!

THE COST
OF CREATIVITY

The Hoffman Family Players walk onto the stage to tune their instruments. David and Kimberly, properly awed by the occasion of staying up late to attend a concert, watch with fascination as the guest artists tune the strings of their violins, cello, viola, and harp to the piano. The instrumentalists assume an attitude of concentration and begin their performance. The mastery of each performer becomes increasingly apparent as the composition unfolds, revealing the unique character of each instrument. The combined talents of any group of gifted people would be noteworthy, but this musical collaboration from a single family—four young adults and their parents—is no less than astounding! Watching this family make music, I am aware of being a participant in an extraordinary event.

Occasionally I glance from the corner of my eye at David, who sits rapt and still. What is going through his mind as he watches the inspired performance of these superb artists? Does he see any relationship between their precision and *his* finger exercises? Can he relate their command of notes to *his* painstaking efforts to connect a black dot on a music staff to a white key on the piano? Does he realize that these children, too, have spent endless hours practicing scales and repetitious exercises? Does he imagine the countless times the children must have begged their mother to let them play outdoors instead of practice? Can he picture the times when these children, too, were in tears, wanting to quit? Or is David merely caught up in the sheer pleasure of the performance?

Surely these offspring of supremely talented parents have to their advantage much that genes and environment can offer: exposure to great music from earliest childhood, fine professional training, constant stimulation and reinforcement of their talents, unerring instincts, and, perhaps, an occasional stroke of genius. However even for the most gifted there is that inescapable and always demanding necessity to develop the basic disciplines of the art. However strong the motivation to learn may be, however quickly the basic techniques and knowledge are acquired, everyone must endure some phases of drudgery to master the rudimental concepts and skills. Surely these young people must have at some time or other wearied of the constant demands for new disciplines; they must have become tired under the weight of their task. Likewise this mother (whom I regarded with envious eyes) must have had to draw on her entire wisdom and ingenuity to see them through those tedious tasks. Transcendant moments of achievement are not the product of talent alone but of years of perseverance and practice.

My thoughts return to David, who has been a piano student for three months. I do not know where his study will lead. I do know that presently, despite periods of resistance or discouragement, his interest is strong and his motivation high. The pleasure he receives from performing a piece with competency far outweighs the pain he experiences in the learning process. Regardless of his musical destiny, this training will not have been wasted.

Certainly I am as conscious of the development of his character through this experience as I am of his greater understanding of music. Insistence on discipline in any area of one's life can lead to self-discipline in other aspects of life. Whether it is the remarkable Mrs. Hoffman with her gifted four or whether it is Dave and I with our three untested quantities; whether it is music or any other discipline, the same is true: when children agree to pursue a goal (even one advocated by another), it becomes the duty of parents to encourage them through the inevitable laborious stages. They must be taught that every discipline—athletics, academics, or art—has demanding aspects. There is a price to pay. There are no gimmicks nor devices to ease stress; there are no shortcuts. Competency must be grounded in sound knowledge and technical skill. Hunger for knowledge and patient endurance are crucial factors in the creative process.

The concert is over. The players pack up their instruments. They have good reason to feel pleased with this evening's performance. They could sit back, so to speak, and rest in their present level of proficiency, repeating themselves indefinitely. It would more than satisfy most people; it would certainly satisfy me. However I am sure that they won't. The same intensity, the same devotion to their art that has brought them this far will carry them farther. They will continue to strive with exacting conscience to communicate the eternal elements of music.

COLLECTION OBSESSION

"I'm ready for a room check!" David hollers from his bedroom.

Entering David's room, I'm struck by an incredible sense of disarray. Bedcovers are straightened and floors are cleared, true, but every available surface is cluttered with stacks of "stuff."

"You've done a good job of cleaning your room, David, but is there anything you can do about all this clutter?" I wave my arm around the room, then randomly select the bureau for illustration. "Surely, you can get rid of some of this junk!"

"Junk!" David exclaims. "Mom, these are my collections!"

My eyes focus from a blur of objects to individual items. Amazingly a distinct pattern of organization emerges from the vast array of articles. In a straight row, along the back of the bureau, are his father's trophies, ranging from high-school years to the present. Stacked in three precarious piles are football, baseball, and basketball cards. Scores of unsharpened pencils, each stamped in silver with the name of a professional football team, are sorted according to national division. One segment of his dresser is devoted exclusively to shell storage: large cabinets, small boxes, individual specimens. Coin folders, coin tubes, and coin books occupy all remaining space.

This single surface is only partially representative of David's craze for collecting. Scattered throughout the room, filling all available nooks and crannies are his other collections: matchbox cars, toy people, balloons, sticks of unchewed gum, empty tic-tac boxes, hats, pencil sharpeners, certificates, and various assortments of allegedly related objects. When challenged as to the need for these said items, David resolutely responds with heated conviction, "These are my collections!"

What explains this collection obsession! Is it an acquisition instinct within him, compelling him to gather treasure like a squirrel hoarding nuts? Is it avarice driving him, like Scrooge of old, to possess more and more? Or is it some subconscious urge to gather together everything in sight and systematize?

By what standard does he assign value? By what measure does he

40

calculate depreciation? For many months he will hoard sticks of gum, depriving himself of the pleasure of chewing them, while his brother and sister snap and savor their wads. Then for no apparent reason, he will unwrap his entire cache, stuff each and every stick into his mouth and chew until his jaws ache. He has been known to inflate an entire balloon collection and pop it in a single sitting. He might suddenly distribute cherished baseball cards indiscriminately or remove all certificates from his walls, leaving only blank space. Has he tired of possessions, wearied of pursuits, or have all these items come to be no longer of interest to him?

How do I explain the power of certain things over me? In my kitchen I have assembled a collection of blue and white pottery that exceeds any needed use. Scattered throughout the house are hearts of every conceivable sort: boxes, candles, paper weights, trivets, and trinkets. I have more boxes of stationery than I do intentions of writing letters. There is no adequate justification for the many picture frames, books, fragments of stained glass, silver spoons, old porcelain, bottles, boxes, pots, and pitchers—not to mention other countless "treasures" that have cluttered my life.

Must one justify such a natural and satisfying pursuit as collecting? Can one explain it? Perhaps we could attribute the appeal for certain things to associations with specific people, places, ideas, or events. Old objects recall the past, whispering of a time or way of life of particular appeal. There is, to be sure, a definite challenge to the pursuit of making a discovery or finding a missing piece. Certain things strike us as simply being beautiful. Beyond any attempt to justify, there exists an inexplicable, deep yearning for certain objects.

Likewise for David there must be satisfaction in surrounding himself with objects he considers lovely, valuable, or interesting. Certainly he derives pleasure from a pursuit and delight from making a discovery. The reasons for his specific choices notwithstanding, collecting is his way of reaching out and taking hold of an infinitely complex world as it reveals itself to him. It is his way of sifting, sorting, and selecting objects from the overwhelming array of facts and impressions that bombard him daily. A collection is his personal statement, his proclamation: This I value. These are important to me.

Walter De La Mare has written, "Collecting is a shortcut to all kinds of knowledge and learning, to systematic habits of the senses. It trains the eye, practices tastes and judgment and is a godsend in an untidy world."

"Why do you collect?" I have asked David.

"Something to do," he answers.

"Something to do," I muse. Something to do, indeed!

WHO'S RAISING OUR CHILDREN?

Choices. . . . Choices. . . . The children are bombarded by choices: Cub Scouts, Brownies, Explorer's Club, Little League, Indian Guides, Children's Museum, YMCA, chorus, lessons of all kinds, and more. Each organization waves its banner and peddles its wares, vying for our children's time and attention.

Every activity spawns a dozen other activities, or so it seems: parties to begin the season, parties to end the season, field trips, fund-raising projects, programs, and practices. From the oldest to the youngest, each child is ensnared in the organizational system. Even Jonathan became a full-fledged "Organization Man" since his part-time enrollment in nursery school with its projects, programs, and parties!

I find myself criss-crossing town, fetching one child, depositing another. I find myself pushing mealtime into one child's bedtime to accommodate another child's ball practice. I find family time being surplanted by organizational time. I find the quality of the children's performance being adversely affected by the quantity of their activities. And dizzy with details—dues, dates, destinations, deadlines—I find myself resisting their overloaded schedule and those organizations responsible for it.

Granted, my feelings are momentarily colored by my inability to keep up with the current demands. Nonetheless such immediate pressures raise issues that definitely transcend problems of mere scheduling. I can't help but feel that those very organizations designed to serve the family can, in actuality, compete against it. And I wonder if all these activities are really in my children's best interests?

It has become increasingly common that functions traditionally held to be the responsibility of the family are being transferred to auxiliary professions and institutions. Just who can do the job the best? Clearly public schools are better equipped to provide a systematic, comprehensive program of study for my children than is any single home. Social organizations offer enriching experiences which the family is too limited to provide. But are there activities, best suited for the family, which I have inadvertently relegated to those very organizations which crowd the schedule and pull my family assunder?

And what about the number of activities in my children's lives? Am I programing my young for general mediocrity by permitting them to assume more activities than they can master? Indeed, must they do everything?

There are so many enrichments available to children and so few hours to assimilate them. Exposing our children to a wide variety of experiences is important to the development of their abilities. But we must limit the quantity of their involvements to safeguard the quality of their achievements. We must narrow their options to reserve time for other things we consider important: time for the family to do things together—or just to *be* together; time to do nothing—or *anything*. If we do not "schedule" the things we value, they will be eliminated by default.

My resistance is not to the organizations or the activities themselves. Rather than rail against these supportive institutions, I must turn my occasion of overextension into that of reevaluation. Husband and wife, parents and children, we must submit our choices to profound questioning. Do the children need a given activity? Who should be providing such an experience? Who can do it best? Is there something better they should be doing? Is a given activity for my child's benefit or for mine?

We must ask these questions, testing our answers against our values. Often such choices will involve the sacrifice of certain things we value for others we value even more. If we do not make thoughtful decisions for and with our family, we will invariably be swept into the swiftly flowing and dangerous rapids of superfluous activity.

I am truly thankful for schools, church, and clubs which serve our family. They provide many important experiences for our children that we would have neither energy nor resources to offer. But we must remember that these organizations and the dedicated people who serve them cannot possibly care for our children as can their father and mother. And we must never forget who is ultimately charged with the responsibility of raising our children.

FIT FOR A CHILD

Parents must structure a home environment that is conducive to the nurture and enrichment of our children.

MORE THAN A HOUSE

A cardinal with a twig in her beak darts into an opening in a thick hedge; there in the crotch of a stout branch she builds her nest. Off she flies again in search of more material. She returns with a beak full of dry grass. A male cardinal with bright plumage, supposedly her mate, perches on a tree limb above the nest, encouraging her with vigorous whistles: "Whoit, whoit, whoit, whorty, whorty, whoit, whoit."

How carefully this mother-to-be constructs a home for her young! Tirelessly she assembles dry grasses, twigs, and stems; deftly she shapes them into a rough, firm cup. With ingenuity and diligence she builds her nest, safe and snug.

Her work is not finished when her nest is completed. She will lay her eggs and keep them warm with her body. When her brood hatches, she'll remove the useless shells, keeping the nest tidy and clean. Assisted by her mate, she'll find seeds and insects to feed her hungry offspring. One day she'll coax them, nudge them, if necessary, to leave their nest. When at last they fly, using wings that are strong and sure, she can rest; her work will be done.

Observing the activity of this bird, anticipating the work ahead of her, I can see similarities between her tasks and mine. Her mission, quite simply, is to prepare a place fit for a bird. She will supply nourishment and shelter for her dependent brood. In addition she will offer the comforts of a clean, grass-lined nest and the security of outstretched wings.

My mission is to provide an environment fit for a child. I, like the mother cardinal, must satisfy the physical requirements of food and shelter for my young. And I, like she, must provide other elements necessary for the survival and growth of my children.

However my children, unlike hers, have more than physical wants. They have emotional requirements for love, discipline, and respect; they have spiritual yearnings for beauty, goodness, and truth. Their supple minds require intellectual and creative stimulation. If these elements are missing in their lives, their minds and spirits will suffer just as surely as their bodies would if they lacked food and shelter.

Home should be more than a physical shelter. It should be a haven of comfort and beauty, a hospice for weary spirits, a hub of creativity, and the educational stimulus for ever-expanding minds. Home environments, like natural ones, should provide the diverse elements needed to maintain a healthy balance between love and discipline, routine and variety, acceptance and challenge.

Secure homes, like sturdy nests, do not just happen. Someone must be responsible for maintaining a healthy balance of stability and stimulation; someone must protect the home from pollution and erosion of the essential elements. Someone must create a safe place in the deepest sense of the term.

Birds build homes of sticks, twigs, mud, and grass. Humans build homes of steel, stone, wood, and glass. Both birds and humans bring elements needed for survival and growth to their shelters. Materials may differ for birds and humans, but parental purpose does not. This purpose is to strengthen and equip their offspring for the moment they can leave the nest; it is to provide an environment fit for their young!

THE SECURITY
OF BEING SURE

"When will our bedtime be this year?" Kimberly initiates the questioning.

"Shouldn't mine be later than Kimberly's?" David asks, angling for a new privilege.

"Why do I always have to go to bed before David and Kimberly?" Jonathan pipes up, not wanting to be outdone.

The children ply us with questions and attempt last-minute negotiations as Dave and I prepare to leave the house for our annual back-to-school summit meeting.

Dave and I depart for the local pancake house. Over cups of coffee we plan the family schedule for the new school year. One by one, we discuss items on our checklist: bedtimes, mealtimes, naps, after-school activities, allowances, household chores, TV schedule—nothing is too trivial for consideration. Now is the time to anticipate and strategize problem areas. How much TV and when? What programs are acceptable? How can we simplify our pre-school procedures? What is appropriate school dress? Sweets or fruit for after-school snacks? Important activities that could easily be squeezed out of the schedule are placed onto the daily, weekly, or monthly calendar: family devotions, individual "tea parties," read-aloud time, family outings.

Walking step by step through a typical day and week, Dave becomes informed on aspects of the children's lives he misses; I benefit from his fatherly insight and wisdom. Away from eager little ears, we are free to reflect on the children's problems and development and to plot future directions. Areas of tension concerning child rearing are thrown into the arena for discussion, giving us opportunity to wrestle through differences and adopt a working compromise.

When our planning is completed, we will enter into phase two: a family council. Tomorrow, during the evening meal Dave will present the plan to the children for challenge, input, and revision. While phase three, facilitation of the plan, will fall largely on me, Dave is indispensable to its success. As an enlightened architect, he can enforce the plan when he is home and will endorse it even when he is absent.

Children, we've learned, thrive on order and routine. They derive a tremendous sense of security from knowing both what to expect from us and what we expect from them. "Routine is to a child what walls are to a home; it gives boundaries and dimension to his life."[4] Routine provides a structure within which a child can freely move.

Routine, furthermore, provides a solid structure on which to build the extra special, out-of-the-ordinary events. It becomes a base for meaningful creative pursuits. Against the backdrop of regularity and order, variety stands out in bold relief and can be appreciated and enjoyed.

Parents, as well, benefit from a routine. After the initial effort of establishing rules and routines, there is more time and energy for personal endeavors. Fixed naptimes and bedtimes secure an opportunity for me to be alone as well as for Dave and me to be together. When hassles over basic procedures are eliminated, we are free to really enjoy our children.

The schedule, of course, must be flexible and subject to change; it is meant to serve, not rule us. We have discovered that as our individual lives become complicated by additional options, balanced living becomes increasingly difficult to attain. If we do not begin with a solid structure of patterns and procedures, the essentials will be usurped by nonessentials.

We have had a lovely summer. We've luxuriated in a leisurely, elastic vacation schedule. Now we are ready to pull in the reins, tighten the slack, and press on to new challenges and new adventures!

MISSION IMPOSSIBLE

"Kimberly, you *still* haven't done it right!" accuses David as Kimberly sweeps the last square on her half of the sidewalk.

"David!" she screams, speechless with frustration.

I stand at the dining room window and watch this small drama play itself out. David stalks Kimberly, pointing out parts of the pavement that have not passed his exacting standards. Outraged beyond control, Kimberly throws down her broom, bursts through the front doorway, rushes into her room, and flings herself across her bed.

"Come in and sit down," I instruct David, who follows close behind. "I want to talk to you."

"But mom, Kimberly's not even sweeping the edges of the walk."

"Sit down," I persist.

David has been hounding Kimberly ever since they were assigned the formidable task of sweeping the long stretch of sidewalk that flanks two sides of our home. I have lost count of the times they have been in and out of the house, David informing me about Kimberly's work, Kimberly hotly defending herself.

Finally I firmly remind Kimberly to do a thorough job and tell David to leave Kimberly alone. I wave them off with instructions to stay away from me and put this issue to rest.

Obviously this was for them an impossibility. I look at David, so smug and self-righteous. Why can't he leave Kimberly alone and attend to his own unfinished business rather than plague her with his relentless "interest" in her affairs? I listen to Kimberly wailing noisily in the next room. Why can't she, just once, ignore David's constant nagging?

As a mother, no single thing comes closer to driving me to despair than to see my children, my own flesh and blood, turning on each other like savage brutes. There is nothing that elicits from me more primitive and beastly instincts than the senseless squabbling of my children at war.

Granted, a certain amount of fighting is a normal, even healthy part of their relationship. As children battle out their differences, they learn what others like and do not like; they determine and defend their rights and boundaries; they develop skills in personal relationships—all of which is training that will serve them well in life. Admittedly their squabbles are often more annoying to me than of consequence to them. Nonetheless there must be some way to cut down the petty bickering that sours spirits and pollutes the home atmosphere.

The current consensus of many experts regarding sibling conflict is to let them work it out for themselves. The experts argue that few children have been permanently disabled by a sibling. To be sure, many seemingly insoluble conflicts have been settled without my assistance; others have been hastened to solution with this warning: "If you can't work this out by yourselves, I'll have to separate you. Take your choice—your solution or mine."

What about conflicts the children can't seem to resolve? What about certain complex and constant dynamics among them that could be damaging to their self-confidence? Consider how Jonathan can tyrannize David and Kimberly, abusing their rights and property. Easygoing and phlegmatic, Kimberly can manipulate her parents and torment her more intense brothers with her very "goodness" and ingratiating "uprightness." David, canny and clever, can undermine his younger siblings, pushing them to an emotional breaking point. Children can be cruel. The childhood years are so impressionable. Can a parent stand back and permit these subtle or direct attacks on young egos to continue? There are injuries other than physical; spirits subjected to continual battering by siblings may be damaged in serious ways.

It is my growing conviction that when children can't resolve their differences or treat each other with respect, parents must help them. However, in a sincere effort to encourage independence in our children, we parents are often reluctant to interfere. Isn't it ironic that adults living in a society with laws to protect people from each other may fail to take appropriate measures to protect their children from each other? Children are no more in a position than adults to mediate in the heat of battle or the chill of cold war.

Dr. James Dobson, Associate Clinical Professor of Pediatrics at the University of Southern California's School of Medicine, has written: "I will say it again to parents: one of your most important responsibilities is to establish an equitable system of justice and a balance of power at home. There should be reasonable 'laws' which are enforced fairly for each family member."[5] He lists boundaries and rules that have evolved through the years in his own home:

1. Neither child is *ever* allowed to make fun of the other in a destructive way. Period! This is an inflexible rule with no exceptions.
2. Each child's room is his private territory. There are locks on both doors, and permission to enter is a revokable privilege. (Families with more than one child in each bedroom can allocate available living space for each youngster.)
3. The older child is not permitted to tease the younger child.
4. The younger child is forbidden to harass the older child.
5. The children are not required to play with each other when they prefer to be alone or with other friends.
6. Any genuine conflict is mediated as quickly as possible, being careful to show impartiality and extreme fairness.[6]

We have found when similar "Rules of Relationship" are carefully established and conscientiously enforced in our home, much unnecessary conflict is eliminated. I confess, however, that when confronted with the dispute of the moment, I am more likely to *react* to the immediate issue than to *act* on the basis of principles that have been thought through and agreed upon in advance. Far too often I jump feet first into the arena and referee skirmishes that the children are completely capable of sorting out for themselves while I overlook the more serious underlying tensions that do require adult intervention. In all honesty, there are times I simply am not willing to enforce the rules or mediate the conflict; it is inconvenient and time-consuming.

On the other hand, it would be naïve to assume that any system of justice, however consistently observed, would remove conflict altogether. Wherever human beings, regardless of age, attempt to coexist, there will be a conflict between individual desires and the corporate good. In the home this tension is compounded as siblings invariably vie for parental favor. At times, no doubt, we parents even contribute to their rivalry, unintentionally fanning jealousy by encouraging needless competition ("Let's see who can finish their meal first") or by making thoughtless comparisons ("Look how nicely Kimberly has cleaned her room").

I'm convinced that keeping peace among siblings is a mission which would test the judgment and tax the patience of the most seasoned diplomat. Treaties are easily broken; truces are short-lived. The goal, however, is not total absence of conflict. Rather the goal is to deal constructively with conflict, recognizing it to be a vital dynamic in any relationship. Just as our children must learn to live with each other, we must learn to live with the element of conflict involved in that process. We must accept with grace and dignity the responsibility to structure a home environment that is safe, where each family member's rights are protected and individuality is respected.

SHADOWED

"I have a little shadow that goes
in and out with me,
And what can be the use of him is
more than I can see."

Robert Louis Stevenson

Shadowed—everywhere I go, I am shadowed. Or do I just think it so? Am I, in reality, not being followed? Or is it true that persistently, insistently, a little shadow—no, *three* shadows— stick closely to my side like extensions of my being?

I steal into the living room to pursue a solitary activity. One by one the shadows appear. To the kitchen I retreat. A stool is pulled up to the counter where I work. One shadow appears at my elbow, another close behind. The shadows talk; they question and expect answers.

It is not that I haven't tried to reason with them. "Mommy needs to be alone just for a little while. Go and play now." I have furnished their rooms with all manner of pleasures to lure them from my side. Bribery is not beneath me. "If you find something to do till I finish my work, I promise I'll play a game with you." And I've threatened. "You should know I've reached my limit, I really have. I'm warning you; you better stay away from me. I must be alone." Reason, lure, bribe, threaten—it's no use. All efforts are eclipsed by the shadow of their presence.

I have tasks to accomplish, activities to pursue that require elbow room. The children, too, whether they recognize it or not, profit from separation. They need to develop their inner resources for entertaining themselves rather than being dependent on others for their happiness. What, then, does one do with shadows?

Shadows, I've concluded, aren't easily banished, but over the years I have developed a line of strategy which eliminates some unnecessary shadowing. My children, it seems, no more appreciate being confined to a room or designated area than I do. However when they are permitted in my "space," they are often willing to accept substitutes for my attention. Formerly for my survival, I would create nearby an "instant activity center" to divert my demanding child; now I purposely stock each room of the house for my children.

Living room shelves, tabletops, and bookcases are stacked generously with magazines and books having adult appeal. In one corner, however, is a table and two chairs—child size. Story books, puzzles, and a water-fall game proclaim: "You're welcome to stay." Behind my large harp are recorders, an autoharp, and various rhythm instruments. A bit of accompaniment never hinders my practice.

Special places in the dining room have been arranged to meet the needs of children. Many a restless tyke has been transformed into a content and courageous cowboy by the wicker rocking horse grazing in the archway between the living room and dining room. A reading chair has been placed near the shelves which house their most treasured books. Each child has been assigned space in the wall cupboards: storage for games, puzzles, workbooks, and other equipment. Art supplies—fingerpaints, watercolors, construction paper, scissors, glue, colored pencils—are kept in the cupboard nearest the kitchen.

The kitchen, too, needs activity centers for little people. Magnetic letters of the alphabet cling to the refrigerator for little fingers to arrange by color or words. On the top of the refrigerator is a large reed clothesbasket of games containing many little pieces. This basket is available on request upon condition that all pieces be returned to their proper coffee can. The stoneware crock next to the stove is filled with miniature vehicles and pull toys that glide smoothly across kitchen tile surfaces.

Around the corner in the roomy, old hallway are a blackboard, easel, and bulletin board. At the end of this improvised media center is an old fashioned school desk, a record player, and a collection of records. A cloth theatre, having pockets stuffed with puppets, is suspended in the arch of a seldom used doorway. On one wall hangs a gallery of the children's masterpieces in gaily painted frames.

No room escapes infiltration. The sitting room is graced with a wide-handled wicker basket stocked with "quiet toys" which will not disrupt serious TV watchers. Water toys are docked in the bathtub; binoculars and a birdbook are near the window in the breakfast room. Furnishing a home for little ones, I find, makes it a much more enjoyable place for grown-ups as well!

There are also unexpected side benefits. The children experience diverse kinds of play when toys are distributed throughout the house. A huge clutter of toys may overwhelm them, resulting in confusion and disinterest, whereas the same toys in isolation have far greater appeal. Interest is rekindled when a toy is "featured" in an activity center. Location, likewise, encourages usage—a paintbox near the kitchen is more likely to be opened than if it is buried in a bedroom dresser drawer.

I admit having an occasional twinge of loss when I exchange my treasures for their toys. It's only temporary, I tell myself. The day will come when I'll walk unshadowed through the house. In place of the miniature table and chairs will be a gracious tilt-top table adorned with pictures, gift books, pretty boxes, sparkling paper weights. I will transform cupboards into file cabinets—have my world at a fingertip. Some day potatoes and onions will again be conveniently located in the crock by the stove. A sewing center (dream on) will fill the empty spaces in the hallway and a luxuriant plant will fill to overflowing the white wicker basket in the sitting room. I will transform our home into a place of elegance where adults are free to pursue their own activities.

Or will I? Might I find the refined decor of my fantasy to be a poor substitute for the tattered traces of children at play? Will I, by then, be trained to view the wear and tear as battle scars from noble duty? Will I clutter these spaces with treasured mementos of days when our lives were instead cluttered with children? Might I find myself choosing to keep books and games and toys in readiness for the time when this home will once again be visited by youngsters?

When shadows envelop me, when all diversionary tactics fail, I must remember: they will not always be with me. Shadows lengthen, then fade from sight. And remembering, I transform my complaints into contentment.

MAKING
A MESS

Throughout the house can be heard the stampede of approaching children. Jonathan and Kimberly halt at the kitchen doorway, take a sharp corner, then race to the "art" drawer. Together they rummage through its contents, pulling out glue, scissors, and tape, flinging them on the counter. Several items drop to the floor.

"What on earth are you doing?" I demand.

"We're making a new mask for Jonathan. The string keeps breaking; we're going to tape this one on."

"Hey, someone help me move these chairs!" David shouts from the living room. "If we can get this furniture out of the way, we can use Kimberly's room for pasture."

I step into the doorway and view the living room. It has been totally transformed for the production of *The Three Billy Goats Gruff*. Furniture is backed against the walls; the piano bench has been dragged from the dining room and has been placed center stage for a bridge. Off to the side the table and record player with an orchestrated narration of the script form the orchestra pit. The very thought of extending the action into Kimberly's room puts a hard knot in the pit of my stomach.

"David, I hope you don't think I'm going to let you mess up Kimberly's room, too! I've spent all morning cleaning the house, and I'm simply not going to let you tear the bedroom apart for pasture!"

"Mo-o-m," David wheedles. "We're not going to mess anything. We just need a little more room to crawl."

Jonathan and Kimberly are now at my side ready to plead David's case.

"As for you two," I continue, my voice rising with increasing tension, "you have been in and out of the kitchen leaving a trail of debris everywhere you go. Look! Look at the kitchen floor." I point to bits of paper and ends of string.

"We're going to clean it up when we're finished," Kimberly begins.

"You're going to clean it up before you do one more thing. And David, you confine the play to the living room. Kimberly's room is out. Do you hear?" I assert.

Three faces that were animated only moments before look absolutely crestfallen. David turns to his brother and sister, "Aw, let's just forget the play. Let's go outside and ride bikes."

"Yeah," Jonathan and Kimberly respond in one accord.

Kimberly cleans up the counter while Jonathan and David replace furniture. I continue my cleaning and consider the action preceding my blow up. What began as a simple enactment of a record, gradually evolved into a full-scale production complete with stage props and costumes. Each new development has brought with it a new mess. It is as if the children follow behind me, deliberately foiling all my efforts at cleaning the house. Surely it is not asking too much to insist they keep the house tidy as they play—is it?

At last I have a quiet home. I can clean and polish to my heart's content. But is this what I really want? I claim home should be an environment where all family members can pursue and develop their talents and interests. Is it possible without a certain amount of mess?

What about my creative endeavors? When I bake, I pull pots and pans from cupboards, spread ingredients over counter tops, pile dirty utensils in the sink to wash—later. When I make greeting cards, the scene is the same. From all over the house I gather bits of ribbon, pretty paper, scraps of fabric. Do scraps ever fall to the floor when I work? Writing is no different. When the muses sing, I surround myself with paper, freshly sharpened pencils, notes, and books relevant to my topic. Completed sheets of writing are stacked on the bed; rejected sheets are recklessly thrown over my shoulder. When inspiration strikes, clutter invariably follows in the wake of action! Along with freedom of expression must be the freedom (for parents and children) to make a mess.

Which is more important: a spotless house or a place where people can work and play? There are times when a clean house might take priority, but today should not have been one of those times. Absorbed in the immediacy of my labors, I permitted a perfectly ordered home to become all important. Anything or anyone that stood between me and that goal became an insufferable interference. How quickly values can be turned upside down! How ironic was my attempt to create a clean house while I polluted the atmosphere with my spirit!

Immaculate rooms are lovely to view. They can be seen at museums, behind velvet ropes and printed warnings: "Please do not touch." A home fit for a child may not be a showplace, but it is a place where one can enter and touch and make a mess!

> What is honored in the home
> Will be cultivated there.[7]

"IT'S NOT FAIR"

"We were supposed to tell the teacher what makes us sad," explains Kimberly as she hands me a long strip of tagboard paper. Printed neatly at the top is this "sad" message: "When David goes with daddy and I can't go." An image flashes through my mind of Kimberly's face, twisted in anguish as she watches the car pull off with David and daddy. "It's not fair!" she sobs as she stomps toward her room. It doesn't matter that she was daddy's "date" the day before; it doesn't matter that she has an excursion planned for the afternoon. She is consumed by the present, and only what is happening right now counts.

"It's not fair!" How many times a day is this accusation flung at us? When Kimberly visits a friend and the others stay home, when David stays up past Jonathan's and Kimberly's bedtime—whenever one sibling receives an advantage which violates the others' "equality-for-all" concept of justice, they shout, "It's not fair!"

Perhaps they are right. There is no possible way we can be fair in our treatment of them if, by that, they mean "equal" or "the same." Our children are neither "equal" nor "the same"; they are individuals, different from each other in many important ways.

It would be impossible for us to treat them equally. The statement "All men are created equal" is a political statement, referring to a single quality for a single purpose. To treat our children equally would be to deny or overlook their differences.

Inequalities exist outside the home as well as within. While one person's situation may have some bearing on that of another, joy or satisfaction must not be based on a comparative measure. To cater to the idea that one child's position should be balanced out with another's position is to encourage a false and dangerous assumption which, if carried into adult years, can cause endless grief:

"Is it fair that my husband may sleep while I have to get up and nurse the baby?"

60

"Is it fair that I must submit to a 9:00 to 5:00 work schedule while my wife is at liberty to order the hours of her day?"

"Is it fair that another was chosen for a job advancement?"

"Is it fair that he has the abilities which qualify him for an opportunity which is inaccessible to me?"

It's *not* fair, according to our children's definition of the word. Life is not always fair. Inequalities and injustices exist that are flagrantly unfair. When our children witness deprivation or bereavement, physical or mental handicaps, or any other adversity, they must concede that, unless there is a spiritual reality which transcends earthly reality, life for many is without explanation or sense.

"Is it fair?" The sooner we get beyond that question and on with the business of making the most of what we do have, the better. Equality is neither attainable nor always desirable. We long ago stopped keeping account of privileges; we refuse to match experiences. We challenge our children, instead, to count on our love and to believe in our efforts to treat them justly. We ask them to accept that we can never keep the records in absolute balance. They are different and will be treated differently throughout their lives. We can think of no better place for them to learn this lesson than in our home where our system of justice, however imperfect, is sheathed in love and tempered by our commitment to their highest good.

TRADITIONS

Thanksgiving Day. I reach into the refrigerator and pull out the packaged turkey which has been thawing for the past several days. Carefully I cut away the plastic wrappings and slide the slippery bird into the sink. I stare incredulously at the sight before me: the turkey has no legs! Our turkey, our Thanksgiving turkey, has no legs!

As family members arrive from all parts of the house in response to my involuntary shriek, I rinse the wrappings and scan the label for some clue to what seems an arbitrary and personal act of discrimination. "Butterball turkey, self-basting, tender, white meat. . . ." There is no mention of dark meat, granted, but shouldn't that be assumed?

Dave reads the print from over my shoulder. Deliberately, as if to one exceptionally slow in understanding, he points out that the label denotes white meat and since legs are *dark* meat, it would only follow that said turkey would be legless—as advertised. The children make several needless observations ("Look! The turkey has no legs") and a few wise-cracks ("Guess *this* turkey couldn't run away"), then resume their play.

"What am I to do?" I demand of Dave.

"What *can* you do?" he reasons. "Stick him in the oven and bake him."

"How can I possibly place a *legless* bird on the Thanksgiving table? What am I to do?"

"No problem," he continues in a maddeningly logical tone of voice. "I'll just carve it in the kitchen and place the pieces on the platter. That's much easier, anyway."

"You don't understand." I respond in cold, clipped syllables. "The turkey is the focal point of the entire Thanksgiving dinner. Turkey *is* Thanksgiving. Carving the turkey is a significant ceremony—a family tradition." Never before have I felt so keenly the importance of this particular aspect of the Thanksgiving feast.

"Well, then—I'll carve it in the dining room," he offers.

I look at Dave in utter disbelief. "Dave! Can you imagine carrying a

62

legless turkey into the dining room and placing it on the holiday table? Can you, Dave? *Can* you?"

"Just stick some parsley where his legs aren't," he suggests, unable to muffle his laughter.

"You can't be serious!"

"I really don't see that we have any other options," he states cheerlessly. "Slice him up or serve him legless."

Tears sting my eyes as this heartless man—father of my children, person with whom I have pledged to spend a lifetime—turns and exits.

I stuff the pitiful bird and think of *last* year's handsome fowl: filling him with buttery herb dressing; breathing in the savory aroma that permeated the house; placing him on a platter and proudly setting him before the family and friends—a beautiful bird roasted to golden perfection. A proper turkey with *two plump legs!* I consider canceling Thanksgiving.

Even as I wallow in the slough of self-pity, it occurs to me that this whole business has gotten entirely out of hand. If I am not to spoil the day for the rest of the family, I must get myself under control.

Holidays are important to a family. Eagerly anticipated, faithfully repeated traditions and celebrations provide an enormous sense of continuity. Major holidays, minor commemorations, each with their own familiar rites and customs are moorings in the unpredictable waters of a year.

How the children enjoy our annual cycle of celebrations: New Year's Day bowl games in ringside seats around the TV; Valentine's Day party following the distribution of homemade valentines to neighbors; Easter activities beginning with the sunrise service, followed by an egg hunt and breakfast with friends, worship at church, and a family supper at home; May Day commemoration of spring and the crafting of May baskets; Fourth of July bike-hike to Bok Tower Gardens for a picnic and carillon recital; Parent's Night on vacation when parents and children switch roles; Halloween carving of a jack-o'-lantern and trick-or-treating in individually designed costumes; Thanksgiving communion service with our church family, then our harvest feast followed by a hymn-sing around the piano; Christmas season with its host of festivities. From New Year's Day to the month-long season of Advent, each special day, each special tradition is a link in a shining chain joining the past to the future.

Each shared experience strengthens the bond of unity that is the family.

Special days are tremendous spurs to creativity. Countless activities are structured around a traditional theme. The kitchen becomes a hub of creativity as children assist in the preparation of food for feasts or the baking and decorating of cakes and cookies. Festooning the house with the colors and symbols of each season, setting tables and arranging centerpieces with a holiday motif is a family venture. Designing tiny spring-scenes inside sugar eggs, crafting valentines from paper doilies and scraps of ribbons and fabrics, assembling flowers into nosegays or baskets for May Day—each is performed with increasing skill with the passing years. The children's musical and dramatic experiences broaden as they participate in programs and presentations focused on holidays and holy days. Their literary horizons expand as they delve into the history and folklore of a special occasion. The creative possibilities arising from traditions are limited only by the imagination. And as children observe and assist parents in preparations, they often launch their own creative ventures.

This Thanksgiving can still be a special holiday for us, turkey not withstanding! The real problem is not Tom Turkey but *myself*. I will abandon my attitude of self-pity and cultivate the spirit this day commemorates—thanksgiving.

> Now thank we all our God
> With heart and hands and voices
> Who wondrous things hath done,
> In whom His world rejoices.
> Who, from our mother's arms,
> Hath blessed us on our way
> With countless gifts of love,
> And still is ours today.

TIME TO BE ALONE

"Mommy, when will my playnap be over?" Jonathan asks softly.

"Jonathan! You're not supposed to be out of your room. Your playnap will be over when the buzzer goes off. Go on back to your room, now."

"I don't *want* to!" he insists.

"I'm sorry, but you don't have any choice, honey."

"But there's nothing to *do*."

I take Jonathan's hand to lead him to his room. His legs fold under him; he collapses into a heap on the floor. "I don't want a playnap. I want to go outside. I don't want a playnap! I want to go outside!" he wails.

Jonathan has resisted his playnap today from the moment it started. He has been in and out of my room with urgent requests: "I need to go to the bathroom." "I'm thirsty." Repeatedly he has called me to his room: "Help! I'm stuck," he called unconvincingly from behind the bed. "I can't reach the pegboard," pointing to a seldom used toy on the top shelf of the bookcase.

Clearly it is time for action. I lift him up, carry him into his room, and flop him onto his bed. "Jonathan," I warn, "you are not to come out of your room until the buzzer rings. You have twenty more minutes to be alone. You may spend that time crying, or you may find something more interesting to do. The choice is up to you."

I leave the room and close the door. His screams build in intensity, reaching a climactic pitch, then there is silence. (Could he have had a cardiac arrest?) Resisting the urge to check on him, I return to my room and attempt to resume my reading.

The buzzer rings. I call to Jonathan to tell him that his playnap is over. There is no response. I call him again, and when he fails to respond again, I open his door and look into his room. Jonathan sits cross-legged on the floor and faces his record player.

He sings along with the record, "Who's afraid of the big bad wolf, the big bad wolf, the big bad wolf."

"Your playnap is over, honey," I announce.

He looks up and states pleasantly, "Just a minute, mommy, I want to finish this record."

Playnaps—while at times children will challenge this inviolate institution, it is, for the most part, an accepted, even welcome, part of the daily schedule. The children have not known otherwise. The moment it became apparent that the children were outgrowing their precious afternoon nap, they were offered the wonderful, but conditional option of a playnap. Taking them aside, we carefully explained to them that, since they were getting to be "so big," they were probably ready for the privilege of a playnap. However, they must prove their eligibility. Two long-playing records would be placed on the stereo. If they stayed in bed for their combined duration, they were then free to get up and play in their room until the buzzer sounded forty-five minutes later. Should they not stay in bed or play independently in their room during that time, we would conclude that they were not yet ready and would resume their "sleep-nap."

In practice, if the children needed sleep, the soothing music would inevitably lull them into oblivion. They then entered playtime rested from the two-record nap. As the children reached the point when they no longer fell asleep, the "record-rest" would be omitted, releasing the full ninety minutes for independent play. Playnaps, introduced in this evolving manner, never represented any loss of freedom for the children but rather represented a gain.

My determination to establish and enforce this admittedly generous period of solitude initially stemmed from my own need for daily privacy. I have since become convinced that the children also need it. Removed from the constant stimulation of others, they are calmed. They can assimilate the day's events and plan the hours ahead. Alone, they are free to think originally rather than to always respond to thoughts of others. In short they have an opportunity to get to know themselves.

During this time of seclusion, the children are forced to draw upon their own resources for entertainment. Limited to the space and materials of a single room, they must pursue activities and explore materials usually bypassed when pitted against other more appealing options.

Some of their most creative play occurs at this time. One day I found David in the living room playing his own version of "checker-solitaire," while Kimberly sat at her table illustrating the text of her "book" and, next door, Jonathan constructed tall buildings from colorful blocks. Other days they might do nothing at all in particular.

It is difficult even for children to find time to be alone in our fast-paced, communication-charged society. Furthermore youngsters like Jonathan who have always experienced the presence of older siblings can become addicted to the company of other children. Abstinance produces sharp withdrawal symptoms! These factors make it all the more imperative to *teach* children the skill of being alone.

"All the unhappiness of men arises from one single fact," wrote Pascal in his *Pensees* "that they cannot stay quiet in their own room." This, doubtlessly, is an oversimplification of the cause of humanity's malaise, but Pascal's point is well taken. "In the last analysis, we live our lives alone." Thus we must learn to be comfortable with solitude. I hope that as our children experience that unsolicited solitude in their early years, they will come to recognize its value and continue to seek it throughout their lives.

A LAMENT

David stands on the front porch with an open newspaper in his hands. He thrusts the paper on the bench and stumbles into the house. I pick up the paper and confirm my concern; he has found and read an account of the accident that claimed the lives of four young children—family friends —one, David's schoolmate.

I follow him to the kitchen where he stands numbly gazing into space. Earlier this week he reasoned, "I don't think we should keep thinking about it. We won't forget them, but I don't think it's good to just keep thinking about it." Now he lifts a face contorted with incomprehension and hurt and says brokenly, "Some things people just can't help thinking about. Sometimes there's a sad that just won't go away."

How do we parents help this child cope with a "sad that just won't go away"? David, until now, has experienced little pain that could not be eased by a chocolate soda. How do we, stunned and reeling by the impact of this devastating blow, begin to explain a tragedy of such catastrophic proportions to our child? How do we make sense of it ourselves?

Images of the almond-eyed, golden-skinned children flood my mind. Four youngsters who, being highly visible in their parents' family-operated restaurant, captured the hearts of our community: lively images, totally unrelated to heavy, closed coffins. . . . Vivian, rushing to our table with a pad and pencil, smiling, tempting us with suggestions of good food being prepared in the kitchen or relating with enthusiasm her progress on the flute. Wingfield, appearing from nowhere with the latest knock-knock jokes, then scooting away to clear a table. Vincent, studying at the corner table or standing at the cash register making change for a customer. And little Winnie, rushing to the door and opening it with a flourish and an ear-to-ear grin.

Four young, productive lives cut short. "Why?" I ask. "Why?" How do I begin to make sense of a world in which capricious fate can strike at will? Any attempt to answer is so inadequate as to be mockery. Stock explanations or justification seem glib and facile against this bizzare waste of lives, against these parents' unfathomable loss! How do I help David grasp a tragedy I cannot reconcile within myself?

Staggered by another's suffering, engulfed by my own sense of loss, the lid flies open on my own Pandora's box of fear and anxiety. Big questions, universal questions suddenly become focused and personal. All that consumes my hours and energies at once seems meaningless and futile. What assurances have *I* for my earthly investments? What guarantees have I for those who are dear to me? Are there any lessons from these children's lives, any insights from their deaths to give meaning to this tragedy, if not justification?

These children, one sensed, lived life to its fullest. The phrase *joie de vivre,* "joy of living," captures the essence of their short existence. The laughing faces and bright, dancing eyes of these four creative, industrious children are indelibly etched into my heart and mind, not to be sentimentalized but memorialized as a timeless reminder of *how* to live. Like them, I have only the present. Am I living it, as they did, to the fullest?

I observe their mother isolated by her grief. Feeling helpless and impotent before another's inconsolable sorrow, I am strangely consoled. There are, already, intimations of the triumph of a human spirit over crushing circumstances. "I have lived for my children," she says. "Now, I will live for the people of this community. I will give my love to you." Even in the full force of her shock and grief, she is thinking beyond herself, giving others hope. Here are lessons to be learned, I sense, if only I can grasp them: lessons of courage and acceptance. *Can* I learn from her?

Priorities instantly fall into place when one is faced with matters of life and death. I went outside today to view with Jonathan a "beautiful bush" I had put off seeing for days because I was "too busy." I've read more stories to my children this week than I have in the past month. I *made* time in a crowded evening for a family supper. When I kissed my children good-night, I held them close and cherished the feel of their warm, human life. Momentarily, at least, I know clearly what *really* is important. Will I remember?

Normally, I wrap routine around me like a warm, protective cloak: things will always be as now. Then death ruthlessly strips the cloak away, exposing me to the harsh reality of the fragility of life. Angry, frightened, I want to gather my loved ones close and withdraw from the hard, cruel world. Yet I know all attempts at absolute security are vain, even ludicrous. "What kind of a world is this," I rail, "where there is no safe place?"

Then my Master answers. "Place not your hopes in this world, which is so uncertain. Set your heart on that which will not perish, spoil, or fade; set your minds on that which holds promise for both this present life and the life to come. Seek ye first the kingdom of God."

Life on earth is fleeting, transitory. We are charged to place our trust beyond material circumstances, beyond human securities, to our sole earthly guarantee: the presence of God. When earthly "treasures" are threatened, our true purpose for living begins to have meaning: to know God, to enjoy God, to love Him forever. Mortality opens a window to reveal a glimpse of something greater, more permanent, than anything we have known on earth. It is a view of immortality, everlasting life with God.

If our time on earth is all there is to living, then life is, indeed, an absurd and unbearable game of chance. But if, as Scripture teaches, there is eternity, a different light is cast upon our earthly existence. We are but sojourners on this globe.

Earthbound, I protest, "But this world is all I know and it is, at times, too much to bear!"

"Trust in Me," is God's reply. "*I* will be your sufficiency. I will not fail you."

When all I love is imperiled, when everything seems unsure, it is to these words I cling.

And now I, slow in comprehending, must teach them to my children. A teacher transmits truths he himself has not yet mastered.

My instinct is to shield David from this tragedy. I can't, of course. Even if I could, what would be gained? Can I hide from him all other human misery? Tragedy is an inescapable part of life. It is far better to acknowledge this fact, helping him to formulate a world view that includes suffering, than to try and shield him from it. How else can he be equipped to cope with suffering? How else can he comfort others in their sorrow?

Home cannot be an impregnable fortress barricaded from human suffering. But it can be, should be, a haven where children can learn to cope with trauma. It should be a place where they can identify and express their feelings without guilt or embarrassment. It should provide a warm, encouraging atmosphere where children feel the freedom to raise the questions and test the answers that will lead to understanding and acceptance.

Together we will face this harsh reality. Dave and I will encourage David to express his feelings as we candidly express our own. We will welcome his questions and share with him our conclusions: there is no human compensation for this family's immeasurable loss. There are no earthly securities to assuage our fears, but there are lessons for living to be learned from dying. They do not justify the losses, but they do, in a limited sense, redeem them. Together as a family and individually we must find ways to ease our friends' pain, to share in their sorrow. We must show them through our love that they are not alone.

No, we cannot shield David from this tragedy. We cannot give a satisfying explanation for this abrupt and senseless end to productive young lives. But we can help him face and express his troubled thoughts and feelings. We can help him acknowledge the existence of pain in a broken world. We can encourage him to translate his own hurt into sensitive acts of compassion for the mother incomparably wounded by her loss.

Oh how happy are ye when death has brought in the presence of God;
Ye are freed from the cares that hold us yet in bondage.

Brahms

SECRETS

David walks dejectedly into the living room and flops onto the sofa. His eyes are brimming with tears.

"What's the matter, David?" I ask.

"Nothing," is all he offers.

"Did something happen at basketball practice?" I prod.

"I said *nothing* is the matter." He clenches his fist to accentuate his point.

It does not require an inordinate degree of sensitivity to perceive he does not want to talk. I leave the room conjecturing possible causes for his distress. He spent last night with a friend; could they have had a falling out? Could they have gotten into trouble? Perhaps he is simply exhausted.

Determined to get to the bottom of his problem, I return to my chair, ready with a more subtle approach. Paging mindlessly through a magazine, I toss out a topic that might touch the problem area and trigger a response.

"How did your overnight go?"

"Fine," he says without emotion.

He seemed fine, even exuberant, upon his return. Something must have gone wrong at basketball practice. "When is your first basketball game?" I try again.

"Saturday."

"Are you excited about it?"

"We don't have our T-shirts yet."

I direct a quick, covert glance over my magazine. His face is a study in misery. "You have another practice before the game; they'll probably hand them out then," I reassure him.

"Oh," he responds flatly.

Could he be uneasy about his first game? Is he uncertain about his skills? Are his expectations for himself too high? Attempting to disguise my concern in an air of nonchalance, I persist with carefully chosen questions and comments. "Did you get to play during practice?"

"Uh huh."

"That's good for your first year," I offer with a tone of encouragement.

"The coach plays everyone in practice," he replies, unaffected by my attempt.

"I suppose he uses the more experienced players for the game."

"Dunno."

"Are the older players hard on the new kids?" I reach for another angle.

"No."

I lower my magazine and watch him for a while. Manfully he struggles to steady his trembling lips. "David, I *know* something is bothering you. Please tell me. Maybe I can help you. You'll feel better just putting it into words. If you've done something wrong, you don't need to be afraid; I'll try to understand."

He responds with silence. A tear slides down his cheek. If only he would express what is troubling him! I am seized with a desire to turn him upside down and shake the problem from him. I can contain myself no longer.

"David! What *is* the matter?" Even as I hear the words spilling from my mouth, I know I have gone too far. Like a shade pulled sharply over a window, an impenetrable shadow covers his face.

"I told you—*nothing*." He jumps up and runs out of the room.

I watch him retreat, resisting a senseless urge to follow. I'm left with the deflated feeling of things gone wrong. Even above my genuine concern for his unhappiness, I am distressed by my poor handling of the situation. More than likely, in time, both of us will forget the details of our conversation, but my *approach* to the problem could have far-reaching effects. My attempt to "break and enter" could be detrimental both to David's emerging individuality and to our relationship.

It is not easy to determine that fine line between probing and prying. As a mother I have a responsibility to observe and interpret the mute messages of my children; indeed I have been the primary translator of their unspoken idiom since birth. But in this case I received an unmistakable warning: "Private. No trespassing." Like an intruder I forced myself upon him; uninvited, I jammed my foot in the doorway to gain entrance. I feel like a trespasser.

Albert Schweitzer has written: "A man must not try to force his way into the personality of another. . . . The soul, too, has its clothing of which we must not deprive it, and no one has a right to say to another: 'Because we belong to each other as we do, I have a right to know all your thoughts.'"

Children need secrets. Once Kimberly, when insistently quizzed on a subject of little importance, shut her eyes into a tight squeeze. "I don't want you to see into my mind," she asserted. Whether the secrets are trivial or tremendous, they have an irresistible attraction for children. If necessary, children will even create mystery or give hidden meanings to things to satisfy this need.

Secrets are an important part of growing up. They are indispensable tools for gaining an awareness of being a person who is distinct from others. When children choose to keep a secret, they assert their separateness as well as their autonomy. It is for them a kind of declaration of independence. One could say that to respect a child's privacy is to respect that child's individuality, and to violate a child's privacy is to violate that individuality.

It is possible that David's right to secrecy was as important to him as the secret itself. It all seems so clear in retrospect, but at the time my heart was at war with my mind. How I wish that I had been an encourager, expressing confidence in David's ability to sort through his feelings himself and break out of his mood. I wish that I had been able to express to him that I respected both his need to be alone and his need to have secrets. Clearly it is too late to redeem this situation. I have no option but to put this matter to rest and pray that the learning from the incident will offset the damages.

I hope that in the future I am able to communicate to our children that their home is not only a safe place in which they can express all of their emotions but also a place where their secrets are respected.

STOCKING THE CHILD'S WORKSHOP

Parents must provide "tools" for a wide range of exploration and experimentation, knowing that in the hands of their children, these tools will not only chisel their dreams and schemes, but will also test their potentialities.

THE WORK OF A CHILD IS PLAY

"Mommy! Come eat! You want something to eat?"

Jonathan stands in Kimberly's doorway, plastic teapot in hand, looking up at me with beseeching eyes. I find this barefooted boy dressed in overalls impossible to resist.

"Sit down," he commands, pulling a little chair out from the table. "Now, here's your coffee. Want some cream? Here's some cream." He dumps the entire imaginary contents of the pitcher into my "coffee."

"OK, now! Want some cookies?" He rushes to Kimberly's play stove and pulls a muffin tin from a drawer.

"May I have a plate for my cookies?" I ask.

Pleasure sweeps across his face. Tucking the muffin tin under his arm, he reaches into the stove and pulls out a handful of plates.

"There you go. You get two," he states, dropping two on the table. "Two for me, too."

"Jonathan, I need a spoon for my coffee."

"Is this a spoon?" he asks, handing me a knife.

"Jonathan!" I laugh.

"Is this?" He hands me a spoon. "I need a spoon too. I'm going to get some sherbet, then I got to hide. You got to find me."

Jonathan climbs into the "oven" and shuts the door.

"Mommy. Mommy!"

"Where's Jonathan?" I ask, looking under beds, in the closet, in the drawers. I open the oven door. Jonathan screams with glee.

"I've got to get lunch ready now, Jonathan."

"I already *got* lunch for you," he protests, peering up from the oven.

"But I have to get daddy's lunch."

"You come back! You haven't finished your lunch!" Jonathan unwinds himself, stands to full height, and states authoritatively, "Sit down."

I comply.

"Eat your cookies," he points reproachfully at my "uneaten" food. "And drink your coffee."

I gulp it down noisily.

"Eat your sherbet," he says relentlessly. He adds sugar and cream to his coffee and stirs and stirs and stirs.

"This is very good, Jonathan," I nod, smacking my lips.

"Now, go get lunch for dad. I've got to do my dishes." Jonathan stands, swipes an armload of dishes from the table, and with a busy little sigh sets off toward the "sink."

It's serious business, this matter of play! Much more than a mock luncheon transpired as Jonathan bustled about taking orders, preparing food, selecting dishes, serving, pouring, clearing, and cleaning. He was practicing and perfecting basic living skills, identifying and manipulating objects of his world, using vocabulary and language concepts, and even testing his power over mother within the safe limits of a "role." A busy boy, indeed!

This child's work is his play. It is his means of discovering the world as well as himself. He formulates an understanding of the universe in which he lives, bit by bit, as he rambles and roams, looking, listening, tasting, touching, smelling. He discovers aspects of his temperament and personality by interacting with other children. Gifts and abilities as well as personal limitations emerge while he experiments with available resources.

The play environment is the ideal atmosphere for learning, say psychologists. In the nonthreatening world of play, children can seek and try the unfamiliar; they can practice and master newly acquired skills. Play provides an opportunity for children to relate to their peers, gaining important social skills in the process.

Toys are the tools that implement play. We parents must stock our children's "workshop" with a wide variety of tools to make possible a wide range of experiences. These should include: recreational equipment, tools for exploring the world of nature, water gear, games and puzzles, art supplies, musical instruments, books, records, and props for making believe. We must supplement standard materials with equipment which supports our children's broadening interests. Then we must stand back and permit our children the freedom to explore, experiment, and experience for themselves.

Dave and I have come to recognize a predictable pattern of responses that our children have to most new materials. This pattern of responses is: discovery, experimentation, mastery, variations on a theme, abandonment, and then rediscovery. The following example illustrates this pattern.

David uncovered from storage a large wooden maze, one I had saved from my childhood. Jonathan and Kimberly knelt on the floor beside him as he experimented with the two knobs that tilted the elevated floor in four directions, thereby controlling the movement of the marble through the maze. The children watched as David guided the marble along the perilous path, past holes one, two, three, and four; they squealed with excitement when the marble plopped into hole five and rolled out to the tray at the bottom.

They were captivated! Upon awakening each morning and returning from school each afternoon, they would rush to the wooden box: "I have first turn!" Chores were neglected, calls to the dinner table were ignored as they huddled over the maze in rapt concentration. Through faithful practice, the children slowly gained mastery until one glorious day David tipped and tilted the marble through the winding labyrinth, past the sixty possible pitfalls to the final destination!

When at last the children had conquered the game, they launched into their own variations: rolling the marble backwards, working two balls at one time, dropping five marbles of five different colors into five separate holes and conjecturing which marble would exit first. Finally having exhausted the possibilities, the game was abandoned. Since then the children independently resume the game from time to time. At times their interest is temporarily ignited by the presence of friends. However the fury of passion has subsided; they are on to new challenges!

Over and over our experience defines our roles: we can provide materials, suggest or demonstrate their possibilities, and offer assistance. Then we must walk away. Children will approach toys and equipment in their own time and in their own way!

The work of a child is play; the "tools" are toys. Let us aid our children in their first careers by stocking their workshops with the same careful consideration that we would our own.

LET'S PRETEND!

Tell me where is fancy bred,
In the heart or in the head?
How begot, how nourished?
Reply, reply.

William Shakespeare

Kimberly marches on a carpet, contrived of two towels stretched end to end, to a footstool placed parallel to the bathtub. She steps onto the stool, hesitates for a moment, then proclaims with great dignity, "I want to be a queen." After that announcement given with all the aplomb of nobility, she steps into the tub filled with warm, sudsy water!

The wonderful world of make-believe! With a towel, footstool, and proclamation a child can enter a kingdom of castles, knights, and dragons to reign supreme. On a flight of fancy a child can extend the boundaries of experience to a point where anything can happen by being anyone and doing anything.

Fantasy is an important aspect of childhood. Through imaginative play children familiarize themselves with the grown-up world that shapes their lives. With miniatures and models our children enact adult activities without fear of making mistakes: "I'll have to do this when I grow up," Kimberly explains as she changes her doll's diapers, "so I'm practicing while I'm a kid."

"I'm going to be a fireman," Jonathan confides, appearing in the kitchen with a fireman's shiny red hat on his head. The next day he gallops through the house wearing cowboy boots and hat. "Watch out! I'm coming through," he warns. He rides off into the open range, calling over his shoulder, "I'm going to be a cowboy when I grow up, you know." Jonathan tries out roles as he tries on hats!

Through make-believe a child can approach and master the problems of childhood. Frequently I overhear the children enact their own life dramas.

"You know you're not supposed to mess up David's room," Jonathan chides his stuffed monkey, Curious George, who stares unblinkingly at the wall. "If you get into his toys *one more time*, I'm going to have to spank you!"

"There now," Kimberly assures Suzie. "This shot will only take a second. See! That hardly hurt at all, right?"

"You're supposed to share!" Jonathan shouts with angry abandon at an imaginary friend. "If you don't share, I'll never play with you again!" There are few problems or feelings that cannot be faced, if not resolved, in the controllable world of make-believe where children make the rules and write the script!

Make-believe, for the most part, is an intensely private experience in which adults are included "by invitation only":

"I'm playing kites with Chris," Jonathan explains as he races past me with an imaginary kite pulled by an imaginary string.

"Oh, hi, Chris," I respond, waving cooperatively to a Chris-like vacuum next to Jonathan.

"He's over *there*," Jonathan points in the opposite direction, "under that tree!" Weary disdain taints his voice. Clearly, my uninvited interference was a dash of cold water to his play.

We parents can encourage imaginative play in many ways. We can stock children's workshops with props that facilitate their penchant for pretending: dolls and doll furniture, puppets, costumes, hats and old clothes, a model barn with animals, toy trains, cars, trucks, boats, and construction sets to name but a few.

Conventional tools also count. Our family pediatrician once wisely counseled, "Whenever possible, give your children the 'real item' in place of a toy substitute. To a child, an adult tool is the ultimate toy." Real stethoscopes, a real hammer and nails, a suitcase packed with grown-up cast-offs (gowns, high heeled shoes, jewelry, purses, and hats), full-scale pots, pans, and dinnerware—the real thing, whatever it might be, beats its plastic counterpart any time:

> But of all my treasures the last is king,
> For there's very few children possess such a thing;
> And that is a chisel, both handle and blade,
> Which a man who was really a carpenter made.
>
> *Robert Louis Stevenson*

Parents can support their children's activities by giving assistance when requested ("Would you pin this towel around my neck? I'm Superman."), by providing necessary materials ("May I have some colored paper and scotch tape?"), and by cooperating with their schemes ("Is it O.K. if we put some blankets over the dining room table? We need to make a fort.")

The world holds all the ingredients to set children's already wondering hearts aflame, but we can stoke the fire by reading fairy tales and stories of high adventure to them. They can add fuel to the flame by responding to the imaginings they chose to share with us:

"What would you do if I rubbed this bottle and a genie appeared?"

"What if we could only use our words once? S'pose we'd use up all our words?"

"I'm a lion. . . and I'm coming to get you! Grrrrr!!!!"

Could games of make-believe turn a child into a day-dreaming Walter Mitty? According to psychologist Dr. Brian Sutton-Smith, research reveals that creative adults engaged in a lot of pretend play when they were children. "It enhances creative thinking," he maintains. "The only dangers parents run is turning out a scientist or an artist."

"Let's pretend" is the password for our children into the wonderful world of make-believe. Let us cooperate with their many dreams; let us feed their fertile imagination. May their fancies soar, stretch the boundaries of fact, and burst into the land of fantasy where *anything* is possible!

AFFAIRS
OF THE HEART

"Mommy, I'm ready to go!" Kimberly stands at the front door impatiently waiting for me to take her to her first slumber party. She is literally armed with an arsenal of the familiar: pink blanket, striped pillow, patent leather purse, and, of course, her beloved Suzie.

Suzie has been Kimberly's constant companion since she was a toddler, accompanying her on mundane missions as well as events of tremendous importance. In her relatively short existence Suzie has acquired a vast accumulation of scars from noble duty. Her soft stuffed body is sagging and stained; her vinyl arms and legs are scratched, nicked, and discolored. The tip of her nose has been virtually scraped off from being transported upside down; only a few eyelashes remain on her movable lids.

Despite all this, Suzie is without fault or flaw in Kimberly's eyes. Kimberly is given to expressions of adoration: "Don't you think Suzie is the prettiest doll you've ever seen?" Kimberly remains loyal when friends are mean: "Some kids say that Suzie is ugly. But they're wrong, aren't they?" In an outburst of devotion, Kimberly once asserted: "If our house caught on fire, you know what I'd do? I'd run in and get Suzie and run right out again."

Little does she know how close she came to losing the very doll for whom she pledged to risk her life! Two years ago Suzie lost a leg which had been in critical condition for a long time. The doll doctor confirmed my suspicion; the damage to Suzie's leg was irreparable. Frankly I saw in the tragedy an excuse to trade in for a new model the old doll which had reached an advanced state of deterioration.

Over a period of days, I prepared Kimberly for the exchange. "Suzie's leg can't be fixed, Kimberly. How would you like us to get you a new Suzie?"

"A new Suzie wouldn't be *Suzie!*" she asserted.

"Well, how about a doll exactly like Suzie—a twin?" I coaxed.

"I'd rather have Suzie," she said without a second thought.

"But Suzie's leg can't be fixed, honey."

"That's OK," she maintained.

"Why don't we get a sister for Suzie? Then you can have two babies," I suggested, holding out for a future transfer of affection.

"No," she said with a tone of finality. Regardless of my approach, all discussion led to the same conclusion: Suzie or nothing.

Kimberly's love was greater than my wisdom. After all, who had lain at her side in the dark of night listening without interruption to her confidences? Who had been her comfort in sickness, her courage in new situations? Who had accompanied her through daily trivialities and the big events of her life? And who, tell me who, could desert such a friend?

Dave and I launched an all-out search for a hospital that would take on Suzie's case, consulting other doctors for outside opinions. All agreed with the original diagnosis—incurable. Finally having called or visited all clinics in a fifty-mile radius, we located one kind doctor who agreed to attempt the impossible. "It would be cheaper to replace the doll," she warned, explaining the radical treatment of poking a hot needle through Suzie's vinyl skin. We insisted that she proceed. It was one happy little mother who was reunited with her baby—poked, patched, and stitched but none the worse for the treatment.

This incident with Suzie brought to my mind an incident recorded in Alvin Toffler's *Future Shock*. Several years ago Mattel, Inc. produced a "new improved" version of Barbie, the best-selling doll in history. Mattel advertised that any girl wishing to purchase a new Barbie would receive a trade-in allowance for her old one. "Nothing could be more dramatic," observed Toffler, "than the difference between the new breed of little girls who cheerfully turn in their Barbies for the new improved model and those who, like their mothers and grandmothers before them, clutch lingering and lovingly to the same doll until it disintegrates from sheer age. In this difference lies the contrast between societies based on permanence, and the new, fast-forming society based on transience."

Kimberly's reaction to her doll is an important one. Our possessions have value; they are not to be discarded or replaced at whim. Not only must we learn to carefully select our purchases, but we must also teach our children to properly store and care for their possessions.

While attachments to particular toys, like all affairs of the heart, cannot be legislated, there are some subtle but significant ways we parents can promote in our children a healthy respect for personal property. Dave and I have observed that *our* interest in the selection of a toy transmits importance to it. A child senses the difference between a purchase made indiscriminately and one resulting from thoughtful consideration. We should select our children's "tools" and toys with care and deliberation. We should ask ourselves several questions before making a purchase: Does my child need this toy? Will this toy challenge my child's thinking? Will this toy further my child's creativity? Is the toy durable? Is the toy colorful? Will this toy have only momentary appeal, or will it interest my child for months and years?

Another vital indicator of an item's potential value is the child's interest in that particular item. This interest should not only be respected, but it should also be tested. Out of all David's requests throughout this year a camera is the single item that consistently recurs. I am convinced that the chances of his sustaining an interest in the coveted camera is far greater than in the other many fancies that have flitted through his mind. A child's interest in an item can also be tested by having that child either earn the money to pay for it or contribute a partial payment.

Our children's appreciation of a toy or gift can be heightened by making an occasion of the presentation of that toy. The anticipation of a surprise or the added element of suspense in a gift wrapped box makes not only for an unforgettable present but a memorable moment. A thoughtful inscription in a new book or a note accompanying a gift ("Because we love you," or "I saw this and thought of you") lends a special meaning to the occasion as well as the gift.

Observance of the Montessori principle, "a place for everything, and everything in its place," not only helps to preserve the toy but also enhances its appeal. It is not sufficient to tell our children to put their toys away. We must provide specific places for specific toys; we must train them to return their toys to their respective places after play.

We should take a long, hard look at the circumstances before replacing a broken or lost toy. Recently Jonathan's basketball was stolen from the yard. The basketball was a toy he thoroughly enjoyed playing with, but he also had habitually failed to put it away. He was keenly distressed when it was stolen, and we were tempted to replace it immediately. Our better judgment, however, restrained us. The sharp sting of loss would teach him more than a dozen lectures on the care of personal property.

Children growing up today in a "throw-away culture" with a "throw-away mentality" need strong parental guidance in the choice and care of their property. Too often we clutter our youngsters' lives with an overload of possessions, bombarding them with one thing after another, depriving them of the opportunity to value and take pride in the care of their possessions.

My daughter's refusal to part with her adored baby doll was a powerful reminder to me of what I had experienced as a child and what I know now as an adult to be true: A few carefully chosen toys mean far more to children than a deluge of "things" they cannot possibly assimilate or maintain.

NO
TRESPASSING!

"Would you tell Jonathan to leave my stuff alone?" David calls to me with frustration in his voice.

"David, can't you share?" I question.

"Share? I haven't even gotten a chance to *look* at my presents yet!"

Reluctantly I follow David into the dining room. The table is strewn with remnants from David's "Treasure Hunt" birthday party. Empty ice cream "boats," crumpled skull and crossbone napkins, empty gold mesh bags are all that remain from the whooping and hollering pirates who disbanded moments before. In the corner of the room amid the ribbons and ripped wrappings sits the *real* pirate, sifting greedily through the loot. He picks up a harmonica and toots merrily.

"See what I mean? I haven't even played that myself. Put it down. Jonathan, you've lost my darts!" The distressed birthday boy begins gathering up darts that Jonathan apparently aimed at the board but missed by a wide mark.

"Oh, no!" David groans. "Jonathan's broken my new airplane!" He picks up two pieces of white styrofoam and fits them into a wing shape.

David is right—absolutely right! Sharing is hardly the issue; this is sheer robbery! Jonathan is reprimanded and removed from the scene; David sorts and straightens the recovered treasure.

I, the arbitrator, am left with mixed emotions. Undeniably Jonathan was in the wrong. These were David's brand new toys; Jonathan had no business assuming squatter's rights. Moreover, this particular incident is but one of many in the constant conflict over personal property. Like a bee to honey, Jonathan is drawn to his older siblings' possessions. Big-eyed, he watches his siblings' play until, unable to restrain himself, he imposes his presence upon them or claims their possessions for his own. Predictably the children react with strong emotions. Certainly they have a right to their possessions, but where does sharing fit into the scheme? Must the children always draw such sharp distinctions of ownership?

86

I try to lower the heat of my frustration with cool objectivity. Mentally I review the Family Property Rights Policy:

1. Each individual's rights to personal property is to be honored within the home.
2. Cupboard and closet space is provided to guarantee maximum security.
3. Parents will assume responsibility for protection of owners' rights, but owners must assume responsibility for the *care* of their property.

In short the children have complete autonomy over their personal possessions. They are not required to share them with siblings or friends. If at any time their property rights are infringed upon, they may confidently appeal to their parents to intervene in their behalf. On the other hand, it is their responsibility to put toys away and to keep them out of the reach of younger siblings or visiting friends. If, for example, the children leave a game in the living room, any possible consequences would be their problem not ours. If they choose not to share a fragile or treasured toy with a guest, it is their responsibility to put it out of sight and reach.

Does this make for a selfish child? Quite the contrary! We have discovered that when children's property rights are protected, they are far more inclined to share. The fact is that children love to play with other children. Sooner or later children discover that playing with frier ds requires sharing with friends. It is my observation that this discov ry is made sooner for the child whose rights are secure. Securit breeds generosity; insecurity, on the other hand, breeds possessive ess.

When I assume responsibility for enforcement of the e policies, I become far more conscientious about the designation ar d distribution of materials. Items intended for general use should be g ven as family gifts. These could include basic art and music supplies, a puppet theatre, general reference materials, and playground equipment. It is unfair to present to a child a gift that was never meant to be his or hers alone.

It is helpful, furthermore, to enlist the children in toy reassignments. As time passes, children outgrow certain toys or become disinterested in them. Periodically I will ask, "Why don't each of you gather together all the toys you no longer use or want, and we'll put them where everyone can use them." This way we eliminate silly, but all too common, hassles in which particulars are irrelevant but principle is all important. We also build an expanding reserve of equipment for common enjoyment.

Children, like adults, have rights over their possessions. The children's tricycles are their "wheels"; their rooms are their private habitats; dolls and stuffed animals are their family; their toys are their personal tools. Any violation of their rights to these things is as flagrant to them as is a violation of car, house, family, or tools to their parents. Surely children must learn to share, but first things must come first. They must be secure in the knowledge that they really have this option. We parents must protect our children's rights just as we insist our own rights be protected!

> When I am grown to man's estate
> I shall be very proud and great,
> And tell the other girls and boys
> Not to meddle with my toys.
>   *Robert Louis Stevenson*

SIGNATURE OF MAN

"There, I'm finished!" Jonathan presents to me his handcrafted birthday card for grandma.

He watches my face as I study his efforts. On the front of the card is a traced outline of his hand. "Grandma's really going to love that," Jonathan says pointing to the "Happy Birthday" sticker superimposed upon the design. "I couldn't get my name right," he explains as I open the card. Spread across the two inside pages are at least a dozen attempted signatures, vigorously crossed out in green magic marker. Through the ink I can discern his wobbly letters—JON.

"Grandma's going to love this whole card, Jonathan!" I assure him.

"I know. Now, I gotta go get a picture to send her." He skips off.

I sort through the articles the children have assembled for grandma's surprise birthday package. Inside Kimberly's colorfully crafted card is a penciled message of love and a snapshot of herself astride a pony. David has penned a more elaborate note in his card, recalling the joy of making popcorn balls together (a reminder for future visits?) and an explanation concerning the insert, "My first peace." The "peace," I discover, is his musical composition entitled *The White Stallion* which he dedicated to his piano teacher. Under the cards and enclosures is a painting in acrylics done by Kimberly, a still life of the calico flowers she made in Brownies.

Looking over the children's labors, I am impressed not only by how much they have expressed of their love but also by how much they have revealed of themselves. Jonathan's diligent, though frustrated, attempts to produce a satisfactory signature expose a sensitive and determined little soul beneath the free-spirited exterior. Kimberly's painting and David's composition divulge areas of personal pride and accomplishment as well as avenues for an increasingly satisfying release of inward feelings. Truly this gift package represents in their labors of love more than self-disclosures. Here are true creations!

Art—"the making or doing of things that have form or beauty" (according to Webster)—has been an important aspect of life throughout

89

human history. G. K. Chesterton has said, "Art is the signature of man." We human beings, created in the image of our Creator-God, have an innate desire to reproduce in symbols what we see and hear and feel. Art provides an opportunity to reflect upon our experience and translate that perception into concrete forms. For some people it is the most direct, most honest means of expression. "I deplore the all too common feeling that the arts are a frill or a kind of cultural luxury," objects Dr. Frank E. Gaebelein, headmaster emeritus of Stony Brook School, "They are not. They are essential to being fully what God made us to be."

This is as true for children as it is for adults. Limited though their expressions may be from a technical point of view, children find in art an outlet for feelings too complex to otherwise articulate. Art provides a constructive channel for creative energy. Artistic activity creates a reflective pause in children's physically active existence. During this time they can observe, assimilate, imagine, and compose—developing in the process an aesthetic awareness and appreciation. Art, for some children, offers a welcome opportunity to excel. Often the child who struggles in the classroom or is awkward on the playing field gains tremendous confidence through artistic accomplishments.

"How can I help my child?" a parent might protest. "I'm certainly not artistic!" That doesn't matter. When our task is fully understood, we parents must admit that we are not only able to help our children but, in fact, are the ones most qualified to help. Our goal, essentially, must be to connect our children with the necessary materials which will permit their creative urges and responses to assume specific form. "Without craft it will escape."[8]

It is imperative, at the start, to stock our children's workshop with a wide assortment of choice materials which permit the broadest possible range of creative expressions. Materials can be simple: paper, pencils, crayons, paints, brushes, scissors, paste, clay, scraps of fabric and wood, hammer, nails, and rhythm instruments. In time, emerging interests will dictate other needed supplies. Whenever children respond to beauty or other stimuli around them, materials should be readily available to allow expressions of those creative urges. When children experience something strongly, they need to be able to express it by painting, dancing, or beating a drum!

Parents are in an ideal position to capitalize on their children's responses by encouraging them to translate their perceptions, feelings, or experiences into some personal expression. Activities that arise from everyday experiences are nearly always preferable to those which must be staged or contrived. When children sway or clap to the beat of music, that is the time to pull out rhythm instruments or to march in time with the music. When children react to the action of a poem or story, that is the time to suggest they dramatize the plot themselves or use puppets to retell the story.

Children should be encouraged to complete the cycle of their experiences by recording their perceptions of them in story, song, poem, or picture. A snowstorm, the first flower of spring, a bad mood, or a humorous incident can inspire creativity. Memorabilia from a vacation might be made into a collage; images from an outing to the zoo might be translated into animals molded from clay. The possibilities are limitless.

As children begin to reveal hints and signs of inner inclinations, we should build upon them, guiding them toward fuller expression. When children tell an original tale, we might prod them further with, "That's an interesting story. Why don't you write it down and read it to the family tonight?" If our children call us to the piano to hear a melody they have picked out on the keys, we could respond, "That's great! Quickly, write down the notes so you won't forget them!" Needless to say, our children's reaction to such suggestions should provide the clue as to whether or not we follow up with paper and pencil.

Children will continually return to those channels of expression which they find most gratifying. Parents should encourage their children to strengthen these areas. Increasing mastery of any skill brings ever growing satisfaction and confidence. At the same time, it cannot be stated too strongly that the emphasis should be on the *action*, not on the product. Few individuals will make significant artistic contributions, but anyone can receive fulfillment from creating.

At what point should a child be given formal instruction? This is an especially thorny question because there is no "right" time. It will differ with each child, depending on the degree of interest and talent. One can safely say, however, that in contemporary American society the common danger is to push children into specialization prematurely, depriving them of valuable exploratory experience and depriving them of the opportunity to pursue their interests at their own pace. Too often w to force our children into our game plan rather than permitting them to follow their own inclinations.

We struggled with this issue when David first became interested in the piano. When he exhibited sufficient interest in music, I contacted the teacher I thought would be best for him.

"Wait until he's nine or ten years old," was his reply.

"Why?" I queried, thinking of David's peers drilling scales and performing annual recitals.

"It's a matter of readiness," he maintained, explaining at some length the emotional, physical, and intellectual development requisite to technical training. "It has been my observation that it takes the young child such a long time to gain satisfying competency that he can easily become discouraged. The older child can gain the same technical skill in a much shorter time and be encouraged early on with his results."

"But he wants to have lessons now," I protested. "What if he loses interest by waiting?"

"If he is really interested, time will only strengthen his desire. If he's not really interested, it would be a waste of my time and your money to insist upon lessons."

How right he was! David began his piano lessons when he entered fourth grade. Interest was high; motivation was strong. By December he was diligently drilling simple Christmas carols, which were to amaze his grandparents during the holiday season. I could not help but contrast his experience with my own. Although I began taking lessons at the age of five, it took me nearly as many years as his few months to reach the same level of proficiency. Furthermore the ultimate joy of making music had been clouded by endless hours of tedious practice.

What is true in music, I'm convinced, applies to other areas of creativity. Any attempt to specialize before the later elementary years usually is not only unnecessary but potentially harmful. It can kill the bud of interest with a frost of discipline. It can likewise prematurely close the doors to other potential creative instincts.

Childhood should be a time of exploration and experimentation. As children work with various tools and materials, they begin to separate mere curiosity from true interest, average abilities from true gifts. The wider the range of materials, the more completely they can test their interests and abilities against the possibilities of life.

"We are a form, encumbered by excess clay, that wants to be released," muses Phyllis Theroux. "Mind, heart, intuition, muscle—our natural powers are more potential than actual and the dream that flickers in the midst of the form is ill-defined. Yet the dream persists, looking for a home."[9] Let us help our children discover their powers—whatever they may be; let us aid them in reaching their potential—whatever that may be. May their dreams find a home!

GAMES CHILDREN PLAY

A group gathers around several boys rolling marbles. A line of children follow their daring captain in a game of follow-the-leader. Two boys astride the backs of their partners engage in a rigorous battle of tug-of-war. To one side sit a couple of young girls quietly playing with dolls. Another child creates a bakery shop on a log, kneading her stiff mud dough. A procession of girls, with scarfs veiling their heads, pantomime a wedding ceremony with appropriate pomp. Other children wrestle, roll hoops, walk on stilts, whip tops, build blocks of bricks, or blow soap bubbles. A line of boys cuts through the mass of active children with a vigorous game of leap frog. One little boy weaves in and out of the various games on his wooden stick horse.

Are these children in a school yard during recess? Are they in a street or a neighborhood park following school? Surprisingly they are not contemporary children but sixteenth-century youngsters, portrayed by the Flemish artist Brueghel in the wonderful painting *Children's Games*.

What do these games which span centuries of play have in common? These children, I observe, create their games with the simplest of materials: sticks, hoops, bricks, marbles—or no materials at all. They devise sophisticated games, structure challenging contests of strength or skill, stage elaborate dramatizations of adult activities without instruction, supervision, or audience. Despite an appearance (or reality) of roughness or confusion, children thrive on the company of other children.

This sixteenth-century representation supports my twentieth-century experience: children's play, for the most part, requires only a minimum of activities or toys contrived by adults. This is exhibited early in children's lives when they cast aside a costly present in order to play with the ribbon and wrapping. This is reinforced at a first birthday party when the invited guests refuse to cooperate with mother's carefully planned games, choosing instead to play backyard tag or hide-and-seek. We parents may give an electronic football game to our children, but they are just as likely to pass an afternoon flicking a football made of paper across the carpet toward "goal posts" consisting of a two-finger span. We can equip our backyard with an expensive jungle gym only to see their preference for swinging from a tree and walking the rail of a fence. We could even build them a tennis court, but they might prefer to play "two-square" with sidewalk and ball as their only props. In short, our finest offerings are often spurned for:

> Some oyster-shells, or a sparrow's nest,
> A candle end and a gutter.
> *Walter De La Mare*

What, then, do we conclude? Are parental attempts to provide children with appropriate toys and equipment unnecessary, even futile? Might we just as well strike "toys" from the budget and invest our hard-earned money in more stable ventures? Not necessarily. Within our means, we can supply tools we think necessary to round out an experience for our children; we can supplement "standard stock" with materials which enrich their individual tastes. These things have a valuable place in most children's development, but we need not be concerned if we cannot give our children everything. We may rest secure in this time-proven equation: a few simple props + a lively imagination = a childhood of play!

THE BROADENING WORLD

Parents must expose their children to a wide variety of people, places, and experiences as an initiation to the rich possibilities of life.

BREAKING MIND BARRIERS

"Some kids were making fun of Luan for not speaking much English. Luan can speak Vietnamese, and he's learning English; so really he can speak two languages, and they can only speak one, right?" Daily David greets me after school with updates on Luan, the fourteen-year-old son of our church-sponsored refugee family.

David's head has been swimming with anecdotes and incidents of his new friend ever since he was assigned to David's classroom and, more specifically, to David's care. His conversation is flooded with the same: "Luan is really good in math. . . . You should see him play soccer. . . . I can't tell how much Luan actually understands. When the teacher asks him a question, he just nods his head and smiles. . . . You wouldn't believe the neat things he can make just by folding a piece of paper!"

Freedom has become more than a word as David assimilates the events preceding the arrival of Luan's family in Lake Wales: attempts to flee Communist dominion; months of imprisonment for the father; living on the move until their escape by boat; sustaining pirate attacks on sea; witnessing the brutal murders of resisters; living for almost one year in a tent, hoping that somewhere, someone would underwrite their ticket to freedom.

Nutrition has become more than a vague concept inserted between himself and the dinner plate, now that David has seen what damage can be inflicted upon young bodies restricted to only high-sugar, low-protein diets. The basics of living, which David has always taken for granted, have gained new significance as he watches this family struggle with the rudiments of learning a new language and monetary system, or mastering the complexities of grocery shopping, enrolling in school, and learning to drive a car. Christian love has become more than sentiment as he observes his church family, first divided over this family, unite in action to assist them toward independence.

What an impact Luan and his family have made on David! His thinking has been stimulated by this older child who scarcely speaks English but who can compute complex math and construct intricate shapes from sheets of paper. His world view has been enlarged by befriending this family who risked everything for freedom. Repeatedly his mind has been stretched to assimilate information far beyond his normal frame of reference.

"The mind is a pattern-making system," explains Edward de Bono in *Lateral Thinking*. "The mind creates patterns from the environment and then recognizes and uses such patterns. The patterns are determined by sequences of arrival of information, not necessarily the best possible arrangement of materials." Exposure to new information, however, jolts the mind from the ruts of the familiar, often breaking established patterns of thought and forcing new and more accommodating arrangements.

The breaking of mind barriers is generally a quite natural process. Such a thing occurs when a child like David is confronted by new concepts from a child like Luan. Occasionally, however, parents must make a conscious effort to expose their child to opportunities which might significantly expand their narrow perceptions. When David was still in second grade, he made this comment about an unpleasant incident at school: "White people are nicer than black people." Deeply disturbed by David's glib conclusion, Dave and I arranged a family trip to the black section of town, which resulted in a more enlightening discussion of considerations other than color which could influence one's perceptions and actions.

Children should be introduced to a broad and deep exposure to people, places, and experiences. Moreover they should be guided in understanding and interpreting their perceptions. Thoughtful exposure to life's diversity elicits questions, provokes thought, and demolishes rigid patterns of the mind. It forces children to alter their world view in order to accommodate new information. It opens doors to potential interests and offers clues to their innate gifts through their quickening responses. Indeed the broader our children's exposure to life's possibilities, the greater will be their opportunities!

FIRST
TRY POLICY

Our family enters the Peony restaurant. Brightly colored lanterns hang overhead. Chinese silk paintings and screens adorn the walls. Oriental music softly permeates the room. The waitress brings us a pot of hot tea to drink while we scan the menu, which boasts scores of exotic entrees.

The waitress comes to take our orders. Dave and I select several entrees from the menu. "What do the children want?" she asks, waiting with pencil poised.

"Grilled cheese sandwich!" they sing in unison.

Dave and I share the oriental cuisine while the children munch their sandwiches and contentedly sip chocolate milk. Our friend, Mrs. Chun, who operates the restaurant stops at our table and looks with surprise at the children's plates. "Why do you come to a Chinese restaurant and order grilled cheese sandwiches?" she asks. The children giggle. "Does your mother make cheese sandwiches at home?" They nod in the affirmative. "Does she make egg rolls?" They shake their heads. "When you go to a Chinese restaurant, you should order Chinese food; you can eat American food at home. I'll tell you what; the next time you come here, you try egg rolls. If you don't like them, I'll bring you grilled cheese sandwiches, all right?" With sheepish grins the children agree to her proposal.

Dave and I lock eyes in silent approval of this ingenious woman, who has foiled our youngsters' attempt to be conventional. Ironically the children, despite their love for adventure, can be surprisingly set in their ways. When faced with something new or out of the ordinary, they can become firmly orthodox. "No, that's not right. We always do it this way." Confronted with the unknown or the untried, they can become staunchly conservative. "I might not like it. . . . I don't know how. . . . I'd rather not try."

Come weal or come woe
My status is quo.[10]

For that reason we have instated what we call the "First Try Policy." Certain things which we consider to be good but not absolutely essential must be tried at least one time. Having faced the hardest part—the first try—with a nudge from us, they are in a far better position to evaluate the experience for themselves.

David's YMCA day camp experience illustrates this point. In the spring when flyers were distributed announcing the two-week summer sessions, David used to balk. "I don't want to go. I'm in school all year long. In the summer I'd rather stay home and do what I feel like doing." Convincing though his logic was, I wondered if apprehension of the unknown was an even greater factor in his resistance. We respected his decision although we regretted his lost opportunity for swimming instruction and other valuable camp experiences.

Then several years ago the children and I happened to be at the park on a morning when the "Y" campers were having their opening-day picnic. David was irresistably drawn into the random play of his peers. He stood to the side as they lined up for organized sports. Wistfully he watched as they devoured their Big Macs. One could almost see a thought process going on in his mind, "I think I could have handled this after all."

Throughout the following afternoon his conversation continually returned to "Y" camp. "Well, if I was at camp, I wouldn't be able to play with Jonathan and Kimberly." (Since when did he so covet his siblings' companionship?) "I wouldn't want to go to "Y" camp—they play too rough." (Roughness has never been a deterrent to him before!) "Besides, they go on a canoe trip down rapids. What if someone tipped over?" (Could that have been worrying him?) I interpret his objections as unconvincing rationalizations for not being at "Y" camp.

That evening Dave and I talked over the situation. After Dave made a covert phone call to the "Y" office, he made the following proclamation: "David, tomorrow I'm taking you to "Y" camp. If you don't like it, we won't make you go back; if you do, you can attend for the rest of the session." Despite mild protests, David agreed. He returned the following evening jubilant; he finished the session, fought (unsuccessfully) for an additional two weeks, and has attended each year since.

Despite reasons for resistance to new experiences, be they preferences for the comfortable or familiar, a genuine apprehension of the unknown, or simply disinterest, our "First Try Policy" has repeatedly been the key to the children's considerations of new options. Acquiring a taste for Chinese food or an appreciation for "Y" camp are not primary concerns. More important than the particulars of food or clothing, educational, recreational, or cultural activities is the attitude being cultivated. Children cannot be expected to embrace each and every option, but their lives will be enriched if they greet life's possibilities with an open, adventurous frame of mind: "Why not? Let's give it a try!"

THE SCENT OF FEAR

"Guess what?" Kimberly dances up to me, her eyes bright with excitement. "Alicia invited me to go with her family to this island for the whole day! It's a wildlife place with bulls and wild hogs and . . . and there's a place called Rattlesnake Ridge where maybe a million rattlesnakes come out to sun themselves! And you know what? The only way you can get there is by driving a truck onto a boat. We get to ride in the back of a pickup truck—not inside but outside—and then we're going to barbeque. They're going to roast a whole pig over a fire. We might not get back till after dark!"

"Where is this place?" I ask, picturing Kimberly and her little friend bouncing about in an open pickup truck filled with rattlesnakes while a thousand bulls charge from all sides.

"I'm not sure, but Alicia said something about the Kissimmee River. May I go?"

"Does her mother know she's invited you?" I question.

"Yes! She's going to call you. Can I go, mommy. Can I?" she pleads, jumping up and down with excitement.

"We'll have to talk to daddy," I hedge, falling upon my classic stall tactic. Kimberly waltzes off, ebullient with anticipation.

I check the details with her friend's mother. Kimberly, indeed, has been invited to a privately owned nature preserve about an hour's drive away. I consult with Dave, who gives his enthusiastic consent. I wait, nevertheless, before giving an answer to Kimberly.

The next day I pursue my tasks, working this over in my mind. Shadowy concerns cloud my thinking. Will the girls be careful while in the pickup truck? Will they be closely supervised on the island? Where will the barbeque be? Will they remember to stay out of the undergrowth? I consider the night drive home on the overcrowded two-lane highway. I want to say no.

Then I think of Kimberly's excitement at the prospect of spending an entire day with her friend. I think of the new experiences to which she will

103

be exposed: a ferry boat ride; a day under the open sky in virtually virgin country; the close-up view of rare, endangered animals; a cookout at a Florida cattle camp. It is an unparalleled opportunity for Kimberly to have a valuable venture apart from her family and yet be supervised by trusted family friends. I can't think of one convincing reason for saying no.

Children's worlds are ever broadening to include experiences beyond parental surveillance and the relative safety of home. Minor choices—mornings at nursery school, a few hours at a friend's home—are being replaced by comparatively major choices—day-long outings, faraway field trips, out-of-town overnights. With each additional option I wage anew the internal battle between an irrational desire to insulate my children with the familiar and the more rational recognition of their need to be exposed to a broader range of life experiences.

Surely there are risks in such ventures. Every time they step out the door, there are risks. There are hazards within the home as well! However children have enough actual dangers to face in life without adding to them the burden of unknown dangers. Parental fear can complicate children's already difficult task of distinguishing real danger from imagined danger. Kimberly's real danger is not the presence of snakes, bulls, or speeding cars; her real danger is my fear for her.

Since Kimberly will indeed go on this expedition, the question is, What will I impart to her as she walks out the door? I am told that dogs detect a scent of fear in humans, regardless of the bravado humans exhibit. Children, I suspect, also detect the "scent of fear" in their parents. Will I dwell on my apprehensions, permitting them to grow into full-blown fears, or will I check them by a determined act of my will?

I've taught the children a little song. We sing it with gestures:

> Safe am I, safe am I
> In the hollow of His hands.
> Sheltered o'er, sheltered o'er
> In His love forevermore.
> No ill shall harm me,
> No foe alarm me,
> For He keeps both day and night.
> Safe am I, safe am I
> In the hollow of His hands.

No place is safer than any other place when we are cradled in the hollow of God's hand. There, nothing is permitted to touch us without first being filtered through His love. Taking my cue from this simple song, I will commit my child into God's hand. I will commit my mind into His keeping. I will say yes not only to Kimberly but also to life itself with all its possibilities. No doubt each new challenge will require me to renew this commitment, but I can face confidently anything when I realize that we are sheltered by our Master's love.

RITE
OF READING

"Just one more chapter, please?" the children plead in unison.

"Well, I don't know," Dave stalls as he checks the length of the next chapter.

"You can't stop now!" David insists. "We can't spend a whole week wondering and worrying about what happened to Danny."

"All right, just one more chapter," Dave concedes.

The children settle in for another chapter. Kimberly snuggles close to her father while David leans against the arm of the sofa and props an outstretched leg on him. Jonathan, who meanders in and out of both room and plot, reappears and wiggles his way onto daddy's lap. Dave begins the next chapter, which I suspect he anticipates as strongly as the children do.

I savor the scene before my eyes. Dave reads the story in his deep, resonant voice while the children bask in his presence, absorbing the unfolding plot. The evening sky casts a rosy glow on the nearby teacart which is set with china, a pitcher of flowers, and remnants from our supper of cookie-cutter-shaped sandwiches, carrots, celery sticks, as well as thick, fudgy brownies.

The occasion is High Tea, a weekly event scheduled late Sunday afternoons. After we eat a light supper which is wheeled into the living room on the teacart, we all settle in for storytime. There are, of course, other times during the week when we read aloud; our goal for High Tea time is to systematically introduce our children to the best in children's literature.

The mutual pleasure derived from a beautifully written story, dramatically interpreted by father's voice is reason enough for such an occasion. Our purpose is even more ambitious. We aspire to provide a rich heritage of literature to our children throughout their childhood years. Children, unburdened by the mechanics of newly acquired reading skills, can give their minds and hearts fully to a range of plots told in masterful style.

Our goal, admittedly, is lofty. We hope to sharpen the children's minds on the thought, wit, and humor of the writers; to raise their ideals by exposure to great people and ideas; to quicken their hearts with life experiences which probe the very depths of human emotions; to fire imaginations through adventure stories and fantasy; to deepen roots and broaden perspective through stories steeped in history; to stretch horizons by introducing new people and new places; to whet aesthetic appetites through beauty of words and illustrations. A lofty goal, indeed!

Meanwhile there are many immediate benefits gained from High Tea. We are bound together by mutual friends, experiences, and places as we read aloud as a family. We smile tolerantly at the foolishness of Winnie the Pooh, "bear of little brain," and count his friends among our close acquaintances. We have accompanied Curious George on his many misadventures from sunny Africa to the City Zoo, U.S.A. The map of Narnia, the location of the seven allegorical adventure books written by C. S. Lewis, posted on our hallway wall represents a land as vivid to us as life. Together we raged at Edmund's betrayal of Susan and Mr. Tumnus in *The Lion, the Witch, and the Wardrobe* and wiped back tears at the slaying of Aslan. Through Patricia St. John's *Treasures of the Snow* we lived in Switzerland, felt the biting chill of blizzards and the warmth of the wood stove fire. Our emotions ran the gamut as we anguished with Annette over her mother's death, ached for little Danny's crippled body, railed against Lucien's deception, then agonized for him when he was rejected.

We have delighted in the magic of words as we meandered leisurely through the pages of beloved books. We savored the turn of phrase in William Steig's *Sylvester and the Magic Pebble*; we lingered over big, important-sounding words in the tiny volumes of Beatrix Potter; we relished the rollicking rhymes of Dr. Seuss! Already in our relatively few years of reading, we have built a family idiom relating our experience to book experiences. "The best nest," as in Dr. Eastman's book by that name, means "home"—wherever that may be. "Time for a little something" means to us, as it does to Winnie the Pooh, "I'm hungry, let's eat!"

Stories, we've discovered, are one of the most effective means of conveying truth. "We learn through analogy, through story," author Madeleine L'Engle states in an interview. "A distinguished writer friend of mine said that Jesus was not a theologian but God who told stories. I think that right doctrine is far more often taught in stories than in direct dogma." Unquestionably, stories we've read which explored such concepts as the spiritual war between good and evil, substitutionary atonement, and forgiveness have given the children deeper insight into these biblical truths than our many attempts at explanations.

Good Christian fiction and the Christian element in secular fiction transmit values and ideals to young, impressionable minds without being preachy or moralistic. Principles implanted in the story inspire noble ambitions and elicit the best from a child. Faults of fictional characters often provoke personal discussions. Reading about the behavior problems of the boys in *Little Men* or of Samantha's lack of integrity in *Sam, Bangs, and Moonshine* makes it easier to talk about one's own character deficiencies.

Observance of High Tea is not without struggle or challenge. Frequently it is superseded by another event; sometimes it is squeezed from the schedule for extended periods of time. Clearly, on occasion, the children would rather watch *The Wonderful World of Disney*, Dave would prefer options which have more personal appeal, and I would just as soon not make the effort at all! At such moments I wonder, "Why bother?" With the twist of a dial the children could be entertained by living color and sound. There would be no resistance from the children, no sacrifice for Dave, and no work for me.

However I remind myself that many valuable things in life are not fully appreciated at the time but they yield rewards later on. We do these things not because we necessarily feel like doing them but because we believe they have value. Mary Ellen Chase concluded her little book, *Recipe for a Magic Childhood*, with a defense for her strong position on the importance of books:

> I feel that I can speak with more than a little measure of authority, for I have spent forty years of my life in the teaching of literature to boys and girls of grade-school age, to high-school students, and, in the past thirty years, to girls in college. I have, in these years, learned a great deal about the minds and imaginations of the young. I know that, if they have been nurtured and nourished by an early love of books, they have far finer and more sensitive minds and imaginations, and I know, too, that girls (and boys, as well) who possess books will live far richer lives than they could otherwise live and will contribute that richness to the communities in which they will become the

successful parents of children. I am even convinced that many of the girls whom I teach, or try to teach, have received a better preparation for college in their homes—yes, even in their mother's kitchens—than they have received at school, provided always that their parents have known how to lift them above what Wordsworth calls "the dreary intercourse of daily life" by leading them early into the paths of books. For through their reading in those most formative years from seven to seventeen, they have become all unconsciously the dwellers in many lands, the intelligent and eager associates of all manner of people. Through their early familiarity with words they have gained a facility in speech and in writing which no other source can give. They will never be bored, for they can always seek out a world perhaps at the moment more desirable than the one in which they live and companions often more real than those close at hand. The value of the experiences which they themselves will meet in life can be increased by their knowledge of similar experience in the realm of books; and the sorrows which they must weather can be made more bearable by the lines of poetry forever in their minds. Every year when they come to me as freshmen, I know at once whether or not they come from homes where books have been thought indispensable and where parents have already made their study in college rewarding and delightful.[11]

Why bother with High Tea? We hope that as the children's minds and spirits are fed on riches of the printed page, they develop appetites for independent reading. Surely they are storing in their hearts warm and pleasant family memories to draw upon throughout life. Even now the children unwittingly answer my question. If a few weeks pass without our "rite of reading," invariably they ask, "When are we going to have High Tea again? What are we going to read next?"

Jonathan squelched any lingering doubts with his recent rumination: "I don't think there is any better mother than you. Well, at least I don't know any other mother who has High Tea!" Perhaps it's not the strongest endorsement of my motherhood, but as a testimony to High Tea, it can hardly be beat!

THE RAREST KIND OF BEST

"Mommy! That's *our* song!" The toddler in the seat beside me recognizes the violin concerto that is being played on our car radio. I am pleased but not surprised by his delighted identification. From birth our children have been saturated with the music of the masters. The eloquent harmonies of Mozart have attended me in my routine cleaning; an overly tired baby has been lulled to sleep with the assistance of Handel; children have bathed to a boisterous Berlioz finale.

"Indoctrination!" accuse the skeptics as they observe a child fitting tinker toys to the festive accompaniment of a Bach Brandenburg Concerto.

I see it differently. Through the years this music will make up a small part of what they will hear. They will be inundated with many other types of music without any effort on our part, but if we do not expose them to the rich heritage of the acknowledged masters, it is unlikely they will acquire the familiarity that leads to understanding and appreciation. It is not so much a matter of indoctrination as it is counterindoctrination.

It is not that I discourage other kinds of music. How could I—I who grow misty-eyed over tender ballads, tap my foot to the catchy beat of a popular tune, respond to the plaintive melody of a folk song? Rock, calypso, blues—hardly a category exists that does not contain music for my enjoyment. Yet rare is the music that gives adequate expression to the highest and deepest and greatest of human experience. Many are the gospel songs that state sweetly and simply my love and devotion to Jesus, but Bach's "Jesu, Priceless Treasure" gives utterance to the unspeakable for me. The finest and best music provides a language to express and experience profound and powerful emotions; it offers pleasure in the most exalted sense.

One *can* live without knowing this music. It is not essential to survival. But might it not be essential to humanity in its richest and fullest sense? Some of the most poignant and affirming testimonies to the worth and dignity of humanity are those artistic expressions which emerge in the most degrading, unthinkable moments. I think of Elie Wiesel's

Night, a haunting account of a young Jew who had managed to carry his violin on the death march through snowstorms from Warsaw to Gliewitz. Crushed against hundreds of dead and dying humans, he struggled free and began to play a fragment from a Beethoven concerto. Wiesel writes:

> It was pitch dark. I could hear only the violin and it was as though Juliek's soul were the bow. He was playing his life. The whole of his life was gliding on the strings—his lost hopes, his charred past, his extinguished future. He played as he would never play again. To this day, whenever I hear Beethoven played, my eyes close and out of the dark rises the sad, pale face of my Polish friend, as he said a farewell on his violin to an audience of dying men.

I have not experienced a concentration camp, thank God, but I have experienced how humanity's highest forms of expression can help us transcend whatever imprisons us. I remember so well that time in my life when my three little ones were five years of age and younger. I was tired in body, faint in spirit, and totally dominated by my circumstances. In one exceptional moment when all three were napping, I surveyed the mountain of unfinished tasks to determine which I should tackle first. With a "what's the use anyway" conclusion, I cleared off the sofa, placed a record on the stereo, put up my feet, and stared out the window thinking my dark, self-pitying thoughts. It was then that Handel, quite without my consent, began to do his work in me; the slow, floating, ineffably tender strains of his *Water Music* soothed and restored my soul and spoke to my impoverished spirit.

There seems to be in all of us a reaching out for that which is beautiful or true. Art speaks to that fundamental yearning. We not only have a need to express in symbols what we see and hear and feel, but we have a need to share in and respond to symbols we could not produce ourselves. Art brings out the best in us; it trains and hones our sensibilities. It is not quite so easy to be content with the mediocre in anything after one has been exposed to excellence.

Walter De La Mare has written, "I know well that only the rarest kind of best is good enough for our children." What is, indeed, the "rarest kind of best" in anything will always be a matter of dispute. Even if works have passed the test of time, personal taste still remains a consideration. But from the royal ranks of genius, certain masterpieces— drama, literature, sculpture, painting, and music—have leaped out and spoken to my spirit. Just as I share many other aspects of my life naturally and freely with my children, I will share with them these works of art. How could I do otherwise?

Together, Dave and I have made a conscious effort to introduce our children to high-quality recordings designed especially for children. It is not uncommon for them to accompany with rhythm instruments a record of folk songs or to sing the lyrics along with the tape of a children's musical such as *Down by the Creekbank*. The recordings of Prokofiev's *Peter and the Wolf* and Saint-Saëns's *Carnival of Animals* have inspired their own dramatic interpretations, increasingly sophisticated with each repetition.

We include the children, when appropriate, in our cultural experience. For example, we purchased a family membership to our Community Concert series, which presents a range of artists. And when the children do accompany us, we generally plan to stay for only half of the performance. It's better, we've learned, to whet the appetite with a taste than to kill it with an overdose! Going out for a treat afterward turns the activity into an event, attaching to it additional pleasant associations. In this manner, Kimberly was introduced to ballet, David and Kimberly to a variety of vocal and instrumental recitals, and all three children to community choral and theatrical productions. It could be argued that the children are too young for these experiences. We think, rather, that now is precisely the time for such exposure: it is still a thrill for them to stay up late and go "out on the town"; peer activities do not yet compete vigorously for their time. The children welcome these cultural activities when we keep *their* limitations in mind.

We do not know what music our children will eventually prefer, but we will make every effort to let them know what the choices are. Should they not respond to the masters, they will at least have the benefit of acquaintance; they will not be uncomfortable in their presence. Who knows what music might strike like a bolt of lightning when nothing else will penetrate *their* needy spirits? It may be the haunting, rhythmic tune of a spiritual, the wistful melody of a folk song, or the exquisitely intricate weaving of a baroque fugue.

More important to us than the specifics of their choices, however, is that they come to understand the wisdom behind this sound advice: "Whatever is true, whatever is noble, whatever is right, whatever is pure, whatever is lovely, whatever is admirable—if anything is excellent or praiseworthy—think about such things" (Phil. 4:8).

NIGHTS AT THE ROUND TABLE

The round, dining room table is set for the evening meal. My parents join our family for a special meal with a German friend of ours. We adults ply our visitor with questions about his remarkable background: his early years in China as a missionary child, his departure from Shanghai at eighteen years of age under Communist pressure, his return to his German homeland. He shares freely about his impressions of Germany when he returned to that physically and psychologically ravaged country after World War II. Jonathan and Kimberly stare wide-eyed, mesmerized by this fascinating man who speaks with a subtle German accent. David leans forward, listening with rapt concentration.

As the evening presses on, the adults shift to the living room, and the children disperse for bed. As I make my nightly rounds, the children brim over with questions bottled up since dinner: "Where's Germany? How far away is it? How long does it take to get there? What is a Nazi? Why did boys march in the Youth Army if they were against Hitler?" Their mouths may have been silent at mealtime, but their minds were active, absorbing information and attempting to assimilate it into their frames of reference.

I tuck the children in bed, thinking of the distances they have traveled in time and place, the bridges they have crossed in culture and race, the territory they have explored of thought and opinions—via people gathered around our dining room table! The children have sat spellbound, as an elderly gentleman related anecdotes from his childhood, reflecting a lifestyle far removed from their own. They have listened to the black minister who stated with eloquent sincerity, "I would never have chosen to be born in the South, poor and black—but I was. It is now up to me to do all I can with all God has given me." They have sat through countless conversations in which people with divergent backgrounds or philosophies have discussed or debated their differences. Truly they are receiving a liberal education at our round table!

We have purposefully made a point of including the children in our

113

adult associations when it is appropriate and convenient. Frequently the children join us for a part of a meal, the appetizer or the main course, then are excused as we continue adult conversations. It is not uncommon for them to linger behind our chairs or rejoin us after dinner, drawn by our laughter or an intriguing subject. Sometimes they whisper an opinion in our ears or earnestly pursue a point of interest at a later time.

Through contacts with other adults, both inside and outside the home, our children have been exposed to diverse ways of thinking and doing. Their horizons have been broadened, their lives have been enriched by talents and interests beyond our own. A family friend, wintering in Florida, set up shop in our garage, demonstrating to our children each stage of his woodworking—literally from scratch to finish! A thoughtful neighbor invited our children to help him plant and care for his vegetable garden; the fruits of their labors were the colorful vegetables which they picked and ate with great pride. They have observed their friends' mother in her basement studio, transforming blank canvases into beautiful paintings. One friend has broadened our children's understanding of music by introducing them to instruments, composers, and their compositions. Another friend led our awe-struck children through his impressive collection of paintings, sculpture, and art objects.

Through the interest and generosity of caring adults, our children have enjoyed boating, pony rides, picking fruit in a citrus grove, and many other experiences otherwise inaccessible to them. Often surrogate aunts, uncles, and grandparents provide the special activities we parents find so difficult to fit into frantic family schedules: walks to the parks, trips to a toy store, baking cookies, making paper dolls, keeping vigil over a bird's nest containing several smooth eggs.

We value, even covet, our children's exposure to and relationships with other adults. We acknowledge our limitations and recognize the invaluable role other people play in introducing them to the infinite possibilities of life.

BUDGETING AN ADVENTURE

"My favorite thing was the Country Bear Jamboree," reflects David as he spears a piece of French toast with his fork.

"My favorite thing was the teacups," Kimberly muses over her glass of orange juice.

"I know what was my *worst* thing," David continues. "Getting lost after the fireworks!"

"Yes!" Jonathan sympathizes. "We asked God to find you. But He didn't; *daddy* did!"

Dave and I sternly eye David and Kimberly who immediately muffle their laughter with their napkins. "Does anyone want to get more to eat?" Dave asks, diverting the focus from Jonathan by departing for the bountiful breakfast buffet table.

I gaze out the window at the fantastic castle in the misty distance. Our Fourth of July getaway has been as magical as Walt Disney's kingdom in panorama before us. I reflect with pleasure on the leisurely activities of the past day-and-a-half: our morning at Disney World, checking into the Polynesian Village Hotel, relaxing by the pool, dressing up and dining out, observing the spectacular display of fireworks, sleeping late in the morning. Already last night's trauma—David's disappearance—has become today's adventure to be placed irrevocably in our family lore.

It has been good for Dave to be free from the demands of work and the pressures of schedules. It has been good for both of us to enjoy the children without the conflict of other responsibilities. The children have engaged in activities they could not have experienced at home. They have appreciated each other's company, unchallenged by the competition of their peers. We have made a joint deposit in our family bank of memories.

To think how close we came to not being here at all! It seems that when I am faced with the magnitude of preparing for such a venture, I'm plagued with a dozen doubts. I think about the preparations for leaving (house, clothing, cat) and wonder, "Is it really worth the effort?" I consider the length of time we'll be away, all the things undone at home and ask, "Can we spare the time? Shouldn't we stay home and catch up on our backlog of chores?" I reflect on the extra expenses and work. "Can we afford such a luxury? Two days away from home and what have we to show for it? Shouldn't we spend the money on something concrete?"

But the dividends, I've learned, are just as certain as the doubts. Time and again, despite my reservations, experience proves that the returns for a carefully designed venture are far greater than the investment of effort, time, and money. Our yearly vacation tops the list in both investment and returns. Traveling to the mountains or the ocean exposes the children to changes in climate and terrain. For a concentrated span of time, old routines are abandoned and new ways are adopted. Children become acquainted with diverse people, places, and experiences. They arrive expectantly and depart reluctantly—anticipating next time, next year.

Second only to vacations are overnights like the present one or all-day outings. On a visit to historic St. Augustine, the children returned to the era of sixteenth-century colonial America. They walked the narrow village streets, browsed in restored homes and shops, and watched the artisans create their wares. A trip to Vizcaya, an Italian-style *palazzo* strategically situated on Biscayne Bay, transported the children to the old world charm and splendor of early Europe. They were awed by the style of living suggested by the magnificent rooms which displayed stunning sculpture, paintings, and other antique treasures. On another occasion, a voyage five miles out to sea in a glassbottom boat introduced them to an underwater world of fish, plants, and coral reefs.

At River Country the children have explored the beauty of the rugged wilderness; at the Busch Gardens they have reveled in the lush foliage and exotic animal life of faraway Africa; at Circus World they have gotten a glimpse of what life is like with the Ringling Brothers' Circus.

Each event from a short excursion to a lengthy vacation has certain things in common. First, each exacts a price from us parents be it in thought, energy, time, or money. Second, the value derived from each event exceeds many times over the initial investment. Who will even remember the efforts made, the time lost, or the money spent for such ventures? On the other hand, the event is lived, not just once, but repeatedly in one's memory. Each new experience, each new impression is an additional ring on the concentric circles comprising our children's expanding worlds!

ADVENTURE WITHOUT A PRICETAG

"We're going to the grocery store, the grocery store, the grocery store; we're going to the grocery store, hurray, hurray, hurray!" Jonathan grabs Curious George, dashes out the doorway, jumps on his tricycle and pedals to the base of the oak tree nearest our car.

"Don't cry, Curious. You're O.K. Your mommy is gone, but I'm here. I'm your daddy," he whispers soothingly in his stuffed monkey's ear as he settles him in the back seat of the station wagon.

Jonathan keeps a running commentary all the way to the store. We pass the bank clock ("What time is it?"), we pass familiar stores ("Let's get a coke at Neal's"), we stop at the signal lights ("Go, mommy! The light turned green!").

The mechanical horse outside the dime store is too much for Jonathan to resist. He hops on its back. "Please, mommy! Just one ride?"

"Hurry, Jonathan! See who can get to the grocery store first!"

Jonathan races ahead, places his foot on the magical mat, and the door miraculously swings open. Jonathan grins over his shoulder at me as he struts into the store.

Carefully Jonathan places Curious George in the cart seat and climbs in beside him. I wheel the cart up and down the aisles. Jonathan spots delicacies lining the shelves: "I need some Tic Tacs!" "Don't forget the Little Debbies." He greets old friends, graciously accepts compliments on Curious George's red cap, and squeals with delight when the checkout person approaches him: "I'm going to get you, Jonathan. Watch out!" He "helps" me unload the groceries and freeloads a ride back to the car.

"There, now. Didn't I tell you it would be fun?" he asks Curious George, gently rocking him in his arms.

> To market, to market
> to buy a fat pig,
> Home again, home again
> jiggety jig.
> *Mother Goose*

Truly one person's duty is another person's adventure! A trip to the grocery store contains for Jonathan many components of adventure: anticipation, discovery, and surprise. Stopping by a friend's home to return a book is for Jonathan "going visiting." Operating a pushbutton can of Pledge and polishing a friend's living room furniture is a production of great importance.

Certain chores invariably draw the children to my side: baking cookies, hosing the porch, running the vacuum. Including the children in some of these activities adds a dash of excitement to an otherwise uneventful day.

"Tickets to Adventure" are free for the taking to parents who reach out and seize the special moments as they spontaneously occur. Dave and I awakened one morning to discover a gentle snowfall. We bundled the children in their warmest clothing and led the wide-eyed youngsters outside to experience their first Florida snow. They packed tiny snowballs, placed them in the freezer, and checked them daily for weeks!

The first year the high school homecoming parade was routed past our home, we rounded up cider, donuts, and hot coffee for friends who gathered on our porch steps for a ringside view. What began that day as a spur-of-the-moment snack has evolved into an annual tradition.

Pulling the car off the highway to watch an airplane taxi down a private runway, making a regular "alligator check" as we drive by a certain cove, letting the children carry umbrellas and walk barefooted in a springtime shower—each of these activities may be, for me, ordinary occurrences in an already busy day, but for the children, each is an adventure without a pricetag!

One child's statement the first day of summer vacation, "There's nothing to do," prompted me to write "adventure tickets" for just such moments. I listed every imaginable possibility: picnic in the playhouse, drive to Bok Tower, ride the bike path, walk to the church to meet daddy, visit the fire station, play in the sprinkler, feed ducks, go "visiting," shoeshine at the Arcade, rootbeer floats at the A&W Barrel, trip to the library, explore nature path, visit pet shop, visit toy store. We survived the long, hot summer with tickets to spare. The children enjoyed all of the activities; most of them were repeated at their request.

Our friends, a retired couple, fondly reminisce about their child-rearing years, reflecting on the challenge of raising seven children on a postman's salary. Highlighting their memories were the experiences they created from their limited resources. They chose to see ordinary events as special adventures, and to emphasize this perspective to their children, they consecutively numbered each adventure. A picnic in the car became Adventure #86; Apple picking became Adventure #365; gathering driftwood became Adventure #753. Recently their teenage grandchild greeted them after an absence, "Remember, we're on Adventure #1,380!"

Adventure is more an attitude than a pricetag. Overnights at Disney World, outings to Busch Gardens are wonderful, true; but they are few and far between. Our budget can't support frequent, costly outings. Yet adventure can be discovered in daily routines, captured in the spontaneity of an unpremeditated moment, cultivated through creative foresight. Oh, a trip to the grocery store will not always thrill Jonathan; this summer's "tickets" may not satisfy next summer's child. Nonetheless I'm convinced that infinite possibilities exist within our immediate locale—if we have the eyes to see! Adventure without a pricetag—what number is coming up next?

HOW WIDE IS OUR WORLD?

The curtains open. A magnificant Christmas tree decorated with dazzling ornaments dominates center stage. Dancers make their graceful entrances to the colorful orchestration of Peter Tchaikovsky.

The occasion? Opening night of *The Nutcracker* ballet. Location? Our home in Lake Wales! While access to this fanciful ballet is granted by the presence of a television set, we have prepared for this event for the past several weeks.

First we read the story upon which the ballet was based, of Fritz, Clara, and the fantastic nutcracker that plays lead role in the Christmas Eve "dream." Then we listened to a stereo recording of the *Nutcracker Suite*. For days the house was filled with the gay tunes of "The Dance of the Sugarplum Fairy," the "Waltz of the Flowers" until the children inadvertantly began to hum the increasingly familiar themes. This afternoon the "restnaps" were enforced in preparation for a late bed time.

Now watching the pajama-clad children sit spellbound in their "front row" seats, I am struck by an additional element of the fantastic. Here in the snug comfort of our sitting room, they observe world-renowned musicians and dancers perform in an opulent opera house. Imagine, with a mere flick of a dial *The Nutcracker* ballet is in our home.

Some Christmas season we would love to go as a family to the Chicago Opera House, perhaps, and see a live performance of this ballet. There are many places we hope to visit some day. It would be wonderful to cross our country, taking in the major cultural and historical attractions; it would be exciting to travel the highways and byways, familiarizing ourselves with the landscapes and lifestyles of our heterogeneous nation. It would be grand to travel to foreign lands, scouring museums, castles, and cathedrals in cities and countrysides. Perhaps some day we will.

If, however, we can't take our children to these places, there is nothing which prevents us from bringing these places to them! Through the television screen they have traveled from the Atlantic Ocean to the Pacific Ocean, from Canada to Mexico, acquainting themselves with diverse cultures, races, and ways of living. Through "National Geographic Specials" and programs skillfully designed for children, they have been guided by experts in exploration of the wonders of the natural world—earth, sky, and sea. They have watched live performances of world-famous orchestras and listened to backstage interviews with conductors and soloists while audiences awaited in crowded concert halls. They have been exposed to an infinite variety of human experience through serious dramas written by contemporary and ancient playwrights.

Whether, in fact, our children ever cross the prairie or the ocean, whether they ever climb the steps of the Cathedral of Chartres or walk the halls of the Louvre, whether they ever sit in the Metropolitan Opera House or the Boston Symphony Hall, they need not be deprived of exposure to these places. Exposure need not be limited by finances or geography. The size of our world—and our children's world—is up to us!

A WAY
OF SEEING

Parents must foster an open, adventurous approach to daily living, understanding that true creativity is the "eyes" through which we see all of life.

THE CREATIVE PROCESS

"Mommy, come quick! Look what Jonathan's doing!" Kimberly leads me out of the dark forest of bookstacks into the open clearing of the library foyer.

"There!" she states with obvious pleasure pointing proudly to her little brother. Jonathan stands on a stool which he has carefully placed on the long, narrow foot pedal at the base of the drinking fountain. By standing on the stool, he not only turns on the water but also positions himself at the proper level for drinking. He bends over the imposing machine, taking prolonged gulps, relishing the jet of cold water he can now reach.

I gaze with unconcealed admiration at his ingenious solution to his problem. Here in this relatively simple maneuver is a microcosm of the creative process. First was a desire: wanting to have access to the water. Second came the discovery: seeing the stool as a means of simultaneously operating the foot pedal and attaining the necessary height for drinking. Finally came the action: placing the stool on the lever, standing on the stool, and getting a drink.

These three stages—desire, discovery, action—are, admittedly, an oversimplification of the creative process. Yet for all the diversity of particulars possible in various creative endeavors, the same fundamentals are found in all creative activity.

The creative process invariably begins with a need or a desire. That need or desire may be felt by the composer who is driven by the need to express his ideas in music or by the scientist who cannot find adequate proof for his new theory. The desire may be experienced by the bride who must furnish a new apartment with only wedding gifts and a limited income, or by the experienced teacher who faces for the first time a racially integrated class. The desire may be that of a thirsty, young boy who finds himself face-to-face with a drinking fountain designed for adults.

The creative process continues when the desire produces discovery. The nature of this discovery, of course, will largely be determined by one's inner resources—natural abilities, acquired skills—and by one's exterior resources—available materials. Whether the solution is the result of chance discovery or conscious deliberation, "there comes a moment when many different aspects suddenly crystallize in a single unit. You have found the key; you have found the clue; you have found the path which organizes the material."[12] The discovery has been made.

After the desire produces the discovery, the discovery must be translated into action. The action may involve research, experimentation, development of techniques and skills; the plan of action may take years of labor, or the action may be accomplished in a matter of hours.

Creativity must not be viewed as a quality belonging only to the artist. The same process that produces a sculpture or a concerto or a poem is continually at work in each individual who remains responsive to the needs of life and is willing to mobilize both inner and outer resources to meet them. The same process that ultimately crystallized into a military achievement for Winston Churchill or an artistic triumph for Michelangelo is constantly functioning in the homemaker, the business person, and the child.

Creativity can enrich every aspect of living; it is an attitude, an approach, a way of seeing. Creativity is, in essence, the "eyes" through which we see all of life: work, routines, adversity, disappointment, problems, limitation. The creative person is an artist in living, taking all the raw materials of life and shaping them imaginatively. The creative person is ever looking for a better way: making order from chaos, simplifying complexity, finding unity in variety, seizing opportunity from chance, finding challenge in problems, transforming the ordinary into the extraordinary, the commonplace into adventure.

Woodrow Wilson suggests that "originality is simply a fresh pair of eyes." Children are endowed at birth with "fresh pairs of eyes"; the world to them is new and wonderful. Not yet constricted by deep, mental grooves acquired by years of repetition and habit, they exhibit that lively, unorthodox approach to life which promotes the creative process. Our challenge as parents is to help our children preserve their "vision" by demonstrating in our own lives what Erich Neuman calls an "openness to the world, an openness for which each day is created anew."

LIMITATIONS

Thump. Thump. Thump.

Repeatedly David aims his basketball at an imaginary spot on the roof, catches it on the bounce, then dribbles in for the next shot. Undaunted by lack of equipment or players, he has devised a series of drills in preparation for basketball season.

Football, basketball, baseball —each new season presents its particular challenge for this child determined to drill in a neighborhood without children and in a yard without equipment. With each season I'm astonished anew at David's ingenuity in organizing space and mobilizing siblings to compensate for these limitations. Trees become bases or goal posts; siblings become catcher and pitcher or guard and tackle. Rules are adapted to accommodate his purposes. The season goes on!

Watching David submit to what appears to be a most satisfactory practice routine, I can't help but think of how many times the very limitations I feared would hinder my children actually worked to their advantage. The location of our home is but one example. How I worried about the children growing up in a neighborhood without other children. I would recall my childhood of street-games, knocking on neighbors' doors ("Can Patty come out to play?"), and I would lament for my children the absence of both the spontaneous play and the easy companionship. Reality laughed in the face of my fears. Not only have I watched the children grow in resourcefulness as they have been forced to create their own entertainment, but also I have seen the bonds of friendship among siblings strengthened as they turned to each other for companionship. In addition to these advantages, the enriching friendship of adult neighbors has become an important part of their lives. The lack of playmates has been fully compensated for by the development of personal resources and relationships. Apparent limitations have worked for their benefit.

I think of the many times I have fussed and fretted about my own limitations. Over and over those very boundaries, rather than restricting my experience, have released endless possibilities. I recall our first year

126

of marriage. Faced with an unfurnished apartment and a limited income, Dave and I traveled the countryside scouring used furniture shops for possible "finds." Could this old box be a coffee table? Could this burlap remnant become kitchen curtains? A fifteen-dollar, oversized bureau, leveled to buffet height and painstakingly antiqued, ranks today among our most prized possessions. Doubtless our present enjoyment of "interior design" dates to those early years when decorating was less a matter of money than of wits. And truly the pleasure we receive from furnishings purchased far and wide, each with its own special story, could not be duplicated with a limitless bank account and a warehouse of furniture from which to choose!

During my first year of teaching, I was assigned to a half-sized classroom and a full-sized student enrollment. Beyond the wall of windows, only a few feet from our crowded quarters, was the construction site of the new educational wing. How was I, a novice teacher, to compete with massive machinery and noisy workmen for the children's attention? I didn't. Board by board, brick by brick, we watched a building grow. Math was postponed to watch the foundation being poured; reading groups disbanded when the roof was begun. With each new stage the procedure was the same: when the curiosity of the children was satisfied, we resumed our lessons. Daily during that challenging year I was forced to draw upon resources I did not know I had and develop skills I did not yet possess in order to capture and channel the interest of thirty spirited youngsters. Seemingly adverse conditions resulted in strengthened pedagogy—to say nothing of one outstanding unit on construction!

The start of a family, likewise, presented new limits and new opportunities. Confined to the house for many hours at a stretch, I began to explore the possibilities within its four walls. I developed interests I have not yet exhausted. Through books, records, and screen I've traveled distances and probed depths which had been impossible during my more active, out-of-the-home years. Granted, many options were closed due to the presence of children, but many others were opened.

The value of boundaries is clearly seen in art. The sonnet, for example, is a poetic form with a fixed pattern of lines, meter, and rhyme. From this exacting structure has emerged some of the world's greatest literature: Shakespeare's penetrating insight into human nature, Milton's profound resolution to his blindness, Elizabeth Barret Browning's out-pouring of passion and love. Thought compressed to crystalline hardness radiates with the clarity and brilliance of a diamond. The precision and power that make these sonnets so compelling must be attributed in part to the defining, refining role of restriction.

Originality can flower from the bud of restriction. With boundaries clearly defined, we can choose to look inward and outward, probing personal potential, exploring the resources of our "space."

> Creativity is more often born of necessity than it is of genius. Making use of the simplest things at hand has more often provided a better life for those who chose to use their ingenuity instead of worrying about what they did not have. An inventive talent could lie dormant for a whole lifetime if it were not for the need of a person to satisfy his longing for food, for love, for beauty, and for a dozen other needs that make him seek answers.[13]

Certainly I have limitations, as do my children. Everyone does. Physical, financial, educational, cultural—whatever our boundaries may be, we can choose to chafe against them or to explore the possibilities within them. They can be painful sources of conflict or priceless spurs to creativity. The choice is ours.

EYES
THAT SEE

A path, a pond, two children, and two buckets—a treasure hunt!

"Be careful not to drop your bucket. That's the most important thing," Jonathan warns Kimberly as he scrambles up the steep bank of the pond. "And don't fall!

"Hey! Look what I got! It's a feather!" he continues, holding up a wisp of white fluff.

"I found something I've never seen before," Kimberly flashes a leaf with seeds attached to the under side.

"I found one, too. I found the biggest one. Here's some more." Jonathan sets down his bucket, drops to a squat position and scrutinizes his handful of seed pods. "Wow! This one has millions of seeds!" He drops it into the bucket.

"Look at all those ducks following us!" Kimberly shouts. Jonathan jumps to his feet. "They won't hurt us if we don't bother them, Johnny."

Kimberly breaks a dry, round puff of seeds from a bush. "I'm going to make a wish." She closes her eyes into a tight squeeze and blows the tiny seed-bearing wands into the air.

"Me, too," echoes Jonathan breaking off a puff for himself. "I'm going to wish I could go to the ice cream par. . . ."

"Sssh, Jonathan! If you say it out loud, it won't happen!" Kimberly warns. "Mom, do wishes really come true?"

"Look!" shouts Jonathan, "A butterfly!"

"There's a feather sticking up in the ground," Kimberly runs and pulls it from the dirt, then drops it into her bucket. She runs ahead and stops at the edge of the steep bank. "Look!" she points toward the pond. "Baby ducks! Little, baby ducks."

"They have red heads," contributes Jonathan.

The children drop their buckets. We sit on the sandy bank overlooking the pond and watch and listen. A yellow butterfly flitters in front of us. "It sort of looks like a tiger," observes Kimberly. "It has black stripes."

"Do you hear the bird?" I ask. "Can you see it?"

On a bough overhead, a small grey bird with a russet breast pertly cocks its dainty head and chants a comical "tweet, tweet, tweet." We can actually see the delicate membranes of his throat vibrate as he opens his beak wide in song.

"That's pretty," Kimberly points to the flowering vines covering the bank below us. "It looks like a field."

"A path! A little path!" Jonathan jumps to his feet and runs to an opening in some undergrowth. "Once I saw a turtle here. Maybe he's still here."

Kimberly follows him. "Come here, mom. It's like a cave. You can go in."

"And you can come out of it, too. Here I go!" Jonathan disappears into the brush and emerges on the other side.

We continue our walk around the pond. The children scurry up and down the steep bank, shouting comments back and forth; "Look at that big bird! It's as wide as my arms! There's a bird with a long neck. It's fluffing out its wings. There's a duck with a green head. That's a papa duck—papa ducks are more colorful." Occasionally they stop to gather tiny treasures to add to their collection: a red flower, a sprig of white blossoms, a brown nut. They attempt unsuccessfully to break a fan-shaped frond from its stem.

They spot a tree with a large limb overhanging the shore. Breaking into a run, they race to the tree and cautiously climb onto the out-stretched limb. From their lofty perch astride the broad branch, they view the pond in panorama. Two big white ducks and two tiny mallards waddle in single file below them.

"Two baby boy ducks," Jonathan observes.

"Are the white ones girls?" Kimberly wonders.

Suddenly, ducks appear from all directions, congregating under the tree. "Quack. Quack. Quack."

"Sounds like they're laughing!" Kimberly chuckles. "Seems like they like us. They're gathering around us like I'm a minister—at church!" One downy duck limps far behind the rest of the flock. "Doesn't look like they care much about that duck, does it?" Kimberly notices.

"I do!" Jonathan states sympathetically.

The children continue their comments as the ducks cluster close beneath them. "Look at those ducks—all green and black and white.

See how their necks move forward when they swim! It looks like straw on their backs. Hey! They lost some feathers!"

"Come on, children, let's go," I call. "We've got to go home and make dinner."

Reluctantly the children back off the limb and begin the homeward trek.

"The ducks are following us!" Kimberly shouts, watching them over her shoulder.

"The big one looks like the leader," Jonathan comments. "It looks like they're playing follow-the-leader."

We come to a little bridge and stop for a moment, leaning against the rail. Great oak trees rimming the pond bow gracefully toward the water, their leafy tips almost touching the glassy surface. Clouds cast shadows on the water. A bird with legs spread wide apart balances on a log in the shallow water—a dark silhouette.

"It's beautiful on the pond," Jonathan whispers with awe in his voice.

How many times a week do we pass this pond without really *seeing* it? There is more here, of course, than we have seen; hidden in grasses and under logs, swirling and swimming in the liquid depths are worlds of activity. Some day, perhaps, the children will explore and probe these mysteries on their own. They might scrutinize handbooks to uncover facts beyond their observations: Why do the trees lean over the water? Do ducks really have a leader? Why were their feathers falling off? With magnifying glass they might examine leaves and seeds; with microscope they might study a drop of pond water. A day could be spent at the base of a tree, observing through binoculars the quaint habits of birds overhead.

But for now, for each child, this was enough: a pond, a bucket, and eyes that see!

A SENSE OF WONDER

Jonathan, stick in hand, roves the backyard with all the bearing of an explorer on a distant expedition. I watch, unobserved, from the breakfast room window as this tyke probes the wonders of the out-of-doors. He walks along the border shrubbery, poking the leafy depths with his rod. Up and down the row he travels, stopping occasionally to examine a leaf or to reach for a treasure on the ground. He abandons the bushes and begins prodding the grass with his stick. Suddenly he sinks to a squat, his attention arrested by some subterranean intrigue. Setting his stick aside, he begins digging with his finger, then lifts a minuscule object to his eyes for scrutiny. Is it a worm? An insect? A stone? Abruptly he jumps to his feet, grabs his stick, and continues his investigation of the earth's surface.

Suddenly he pivots in position, lifting a face alight with curiosity toward the tangerine tree. With quick, darting eyes he scans the boughs overhead. What does he hear? A scolding squirrel? The staccato tap, tap, tapping of a woodpecker? A birdsong? Tucking his stick securely under his arm, he runs to the tree and begins to climb, testing each limb as he advances, skillfully and confidently—higher, higher, higher. Seemingly satisfied with his quest, he situates himself comfortably into a forked notch in the trunk and settles back to survey the vista below. Explorer in denim, Balboa of Backyard, what do you see from your lofty lookout? What discoveries do you make from your perilous perch?

Wonder, amazement, awe—such are characteristic signatures of childhood. Children, novice to their ever-changing world, are alert, aware, and alive to the natural bounty constantly being revealed. "Come quickly!" David calls. "It's amazing! You may never see this again. A spider is wrapping a fly in his web!"

On another occasion Kimberly rushes to my side, cradling in her hand a stone glittering with mica. "I'm going to put this with my collection of beautiful things," she confides. The children have spent many a morning prowling about the sprawling root system bulging from the earth at the

132

base of our oak trees. The children examine pockets filled with hidden treasures of velvety moss, hard-hooded acorns, or an army of ants.

"If I had influence with the good fairy who is supposed to preside over the christening of all children" declares Rachel Carson, "I should ask that her gift to each child in the world be a sense of wonder so indestructible that it would last throughout life, as an unfailing antidote against the boredom and disenchantments of later years, the sterile preoccupation with things that are artificial, the alienation from the sources of our strength."[14] For children to keep alive their innate wonder and curiosity without aid from the "fairies," they need, she maintains, the companionship of at least one adult to share in their explorations, rediscovering with them the joy, excitement, and mystery of the world:

> I sincerely believe that for the child, and for the parent seeking to guide him, it is not half so important to *know* as to *feel*. If facts are the seeds that later produce knowledge and wisdom, then the emotions and the impressions of the senses are the fertile soil in which the seeds must grow. The years of early childhood are the time to prepare the soil. Once the emotions have been aroused—a sense of the beautiful, the excitement of the new and the unknown, a feeling of sympathy, pity, admiration or love—then we wish for knowledge about the object of our emotional response. Once found, it has lasting meaning. It is more important to pave the way for a child to want to know than to put him on a diet of facts he is not ready to assimilate.[15]

I was blessed to have parents who did notice, who initiated me early to a life of exploration and discovery. Mother and father both "prepared the soil," but mother in particular brought to my awareness the minute details of everyday living, for she was, it seemed, always there. In my early memories are those of walks along a brook, investigating together the mossy banks or of listening to the laughing gurgle of sparkling water spilling over rocks or of discovering a clump of violets, a bed of forget-me-nots or, should we be so fortunate, a Jack-in-the-Pulpit! It was mother who called me to the window to observe rain advancing like a mighty regiment across a dark, sullen lake, closer, closer, until we were overtaken and could hear the torrents pelting the roof above us. When the fury of the storm subsided, mother watched from the window as I played in the rain, running to jump in puddles formed on the patio, wading in mud that oozed through my toes.

Summer bedtime was determined by the setting sun. My brother and I would sit on lawn chairs on still, sultry evenings and watch the sun slowly sink below the horizon. We would wish with all our might for it to stop in order to stall that inevitable bedtime. Did our parents purpose-fully enlist that visual "Taps" to expose us, night after night, to glorious displays of colorful, summer skies illumined by the retreating sun?

Changing seasons were a never-ending cause for celebration, bidding the old farewell, welcoming the new. The first crocus poking its colorful head through the snow, the first robin with its unmistakable red breast—each was an event, an inauguration of a new season. Our family had an annual ritual which we called "The Tour of the Yard." When bushes and plants were blooming in springtime profusion, mother led us through the entire yard, stopping to name each plant, exulting in the miracle of its loveliness. Her attempts to identify and reproduce the summer songs of birds were a source of merriment to her irreverent family, but, to this day, my attention is immediately arrested by the quail's lilting "bob-white" or the extravagant mimicry of the mock-ingbird. Autumn meant raking great mounds of leaves, leaping into their colorful embrace, and savoring the smell of crisply burning bonfires. When the tree's color reached its peak, father took us "on tour," seeking out back roads whose trees were ablaze with brilliant reds, oranges, and golds. He solemnized the first snow of winter by building a roaring fire—so cold without, so warm within!

> Sing a song of seasons!
> Something bright in all!
> Flowers in the summer,
> Fires in the fall!
> *Robert Louis Stevenson*

Mother encouraged us to employ all our senses: lifting a seashell to our ears "to hear the sea," brushing the furry puff of a pussy willow against a cheek, breathing deep draughts of fragrance from the arbor heavy with Paul Scarlett roses, plucking a taste of mint from the creek bank. We watched with her the miracle of our dogwood tree grow from bud to leaf and blossom. Then, from the tree in full bloom, she cut sprays of pink-flowering branches for us to proudly present to our teachers.

Books, both cover and content, captured mother's attention. She loved the feel of a book—new books with stiff bindings and smooth pages, old books, yellowed with age. Words, she believed, gave clothing to feelings and thought; she sought to dress each experience in just the right garments. Today, when I swing a child, I mouth in rhythm with each push the words of Robert Louis Stevenson quoted to me as a child:

> How do you like to go up in a swing,
> Up in the air so blue?
> Oh, I do think it the pleasantest thing
> Ever a child can do!

I cannot feel the rush of wind whipping my face or see clothing billowing on an outdoor line without hearing from her voice the words of Christina Rosetti,

> Who has seen the wind?
> Neither I nor you;
> But when the leaves hang trembling,
> The wind is passing through.

It was mother's conviction that nothing of beauty or loveliness, excellence or nobility should be passed unnoticed. From awareness of things simple or fleeting to those profound and lasting, she launched me on an adventure of wonderment and awe.

A sense of wonder—the facility to see, feel, respond to the riches of this world. What can I say to commend it? There is for those who "see" a beauty and mystery in the living and inanimate, the actual and symbolic. That beauty reaffirms life, renews strength, rejuvenates spirits and, when all seems to fail, serves as a reminder and promise of something better. I cannot explain *how* it works, only that it does.

My children and I walk hand in hand, so to speak, on a pilgrimage of wonder. Truly, we walk as peers—I aiding them, they teaching me— fellow travelers on an expedition, a joint venture in the discovery of this wonderful world!

MAKING OF A MIND

There are people in this world who chance across the "story" that becomes the novel, stumble upon the equation that becomes the theorum, overhear the tune that becomes the symphony. In an incongruity they see a cartoon; in a child's jingle they hear a commercial; they follow a hunch and find a major newsbreak. They see curtains in a castoff, a souffle in leftovers, a centerpiece in a weed. From a cloud they conceive a painting; from scrap metal they produce an invention.

Why do certain people make discoveries and gain opportunities that seem unattainable to others? Is it chance or luck or superior intelligence? It could be any of these. More often, however, the deciding difference between "making the discovery" or "just missing it" is an active, inquisitive mind, ever searching for relationships, ever seeking hidden likeness. "It is the highly inquiring mind," claims Jacob Bronowski, "which seizes the chance and turns what was an accident into something providential." It is not only a matter of luck or intelligence but a way of thinking, the "mind" one brings to everything.

A child's mind, at start, is eager and curious. How do parents help their children develop their minds into inquiring instruments which ask the questions, which make the observations, which "seize the chance" and turn it to opportunity? How do we help children develop fully their mental capacity? What goes into the "making of a mind"?

At the heart of the thinking process is a continual asking of questions and testing of answers. Parents' responses to young children's insistent "Why?" may be the determining factor in cultivating the habit of inquiry so crucial to the developing mind. An habitual "I don't know," or "Hush, I'm busy now" may lead to a dead-end street whereas "Good question!" or "Let's look that up" may lead to a freeway to learning.

Our reaction to children's observations and speculations turn on either the red light or the green light to further discussion. One day Kimberly commented to Jonathan that before he was born, he was inside mommy's tummy. "Jonathan, when we were little we were *inside*

136

mommy!" Jonathan earnestly replied, "Yes, and when *I'm* big, she'll be inside *me!*" Kimberly and I exploded with laughter. Jonathan buried his head in a pillow and cried with chagrin . . . red light, end of discussion. A similar conversation with Kimberly, handled more sensitively, led us to the World Book Encyclopedia and to an enlightening discussion as we studied fascinating overlays of the human body . . . green light.

Our own observations and queries stimulate children's curiosity, provoking them to further questioning: "Wonder what that bird will do with that piece of string? . . . Do you suppose that's a planet or a star? . . . *Why* do you think he misbehaves in class? . . . How do you guess he feels? . . . What would you do if you were the teacher? . . . Where do you think that ship is going? . . . What might it be carrying?" "How's," "why's, and "what if's" must be encouraged throughout our casual conversations. "To be surprised, to wonder is to begin to understand," writes Jose Ortega y Gasset.

We must lead children from merely asking questions and accumulating information to the quest for truth. They need to develop the skill of discernment that separates truth from error, that distinguishes incidentals from enormities. We must include them in adult discussions, respecting their opinions, while urging them to evaluate and test their ideas. Their minds must consider not only that which supports their thinking but also that which opposes it. We might ask, "What reasons could one have for a different opinion? What evidence do you have for your position?" We must enlist children in making decisions; we must seek their opinion. Children who are engaged in the conflict of alternatives—in food, clothing, geographical location, political ideology, religious dogma—and who are guided by an honest, prudent adult, expand in their ability to discern.

Independence in thought inevitably emerges from discernment. It is a parent's challenge to respond to possible dissent with both wisdom and understanding. "Could it be done differently? Is there a better way?" These are questions we must welcome, even encourage from our children. We must tolerate dissent from others whether in world view, lifestyle, or art.

Children's minds should be stretched and elevated by visions of greatness. Exposure to many forms of excellence in life and in art will assuredly raise their standards and motivations. Great books introduce children to great ideas and to great people. John Ruskin writes:

> We may, by good fortune, obtain a glimpse of a great poet, and hear the sound of his voice; or put a question to a man of science, and be answered good humoredly. We may intrude ten minutes' talk on a cabinet minister, answered probably with words worse than silence, being deceptive; or snatch, once or twice in our lives, the privilege of throwing a bouquet in the path of a Princess, or arresting the kind glance of a Queen. And yet these momentary chances we covet while, meantime, there is a society continually open to us, of people who will talk to us as long as we like, whatever our rank or occupation;—talk to us in the best words they can choose, and of the things nearest their hearts.[16]

Habit of inquiry, the skill of discernment, independence of thought, and visions of greatness—are these but lofty ideals to set before our children? Do they not demand too much from parents who have, after all, far more practical concerns than the "making of minds"? Granted, these qualities are difficult, perhaps impossible to impart if they are isolated goals for our children. But if we parents exhibit them in our lives, children will quite unconsciously absorb and assimilate them into their own.

I advocate "inquiry," but do I demonstrate curiosity; do I quest after knowledge? I advocate "discernment," but do I test the validity of answers? Does loyalty to my cherished opinions stand in the way of truth? I advocate "independent thinking," but do I tolerate another's dissent? Do I resist new ideas of others? Do I risk my own? I advocate "excellence," but am I content with mediocrity? Do I rest in the "status quo" or am I pursuing new challenges? What about the achievements of others? Do they inspire or threaten me? In short, does my manner of living endorse or contradict my manner of speaking? All words pale against the impact of a life!

What goes into the making of a mind? What influences children's ways of thinking and seeing? Many, many things, indeed, but none is more influential than the example of their own parents.

A CHILD'S WORTH

Parents must build in their children the strong ego and indomitable spirit which is foundational to confident, creative expression.

THE MEASURE
OF WORTH

David climbs into the back seat of the car and slams shut the door. "Mike was chosen to be elf, but I haven't given up yet. If he doesn't keep his grades up, they won't let him participate."

"Is that what the teacher said?" I ask, wanting to keep the facts straight.

"Well, that's what she'll do," he confidently responds.

"Is Mike having problems with his work?"

"Not now—but he could," he says wistfully.

I glance over my shoulder at the boy who has been hoping against hope to represent his class on the Christmas parade float. Frankly I'm relieved this all-consuming issue has been settled.

A long two weeks ago David enthusiastically announced that a child would be elected from each class to ride on the school float. His daily, blow by blow accounts of the shifting political scene has given me a distinct mental image of David going about school, campaigning for class elf.

On the day of the election David optimistically confided, "I think I'm going to be elf. I know that at least four, maybe five people voted for me. Michael says Bobby voted for him, but Bobby says he really voted for me, but just *told* Mike he voted for him."

"How do you know who voted for you?" I questioned.

"I asked people who they voted for."

Sensing his political fortunes to be on precarious ground, I tried to pave the way for possible defeat. "David, you're such a big boy; I wonder if it's a good idea to have someone your size as elf?"

"That doesn't matter at all," he responded, not convinced by my observation.

"It would be nice for Mike to be elf. You're successful in so many things—schoolwork, sports—"

"So is Mike," he interrupted.

The moment I've feared has arrived. In spite of David's claim of holding out for Michael's scholastic elimination, his posture is not convincing. Clearly there is one disappointed boy in the back seat!

Let's face it; David is not elf material. Under normal circumstances the very thought of this big, broad-shouldered lad decked out in an elf suit would be enough to move the entire family to hilarious laughter. However these are not "normal circumstances." The thrill of riding in the Christmas parade, I'm certain, is not nearly as important to David as the status accorded the one chosen by the class to be their representative. For this honor David was willing to shelve his masculine image and don an elf costume; for this he was willing to lay his heart bare by blatantly "running" for class elf.

Oh, it's a small defeat, really. This alone is not going to make or break his self-confidence, but life is made up of just such incidents that daily strengthen or weaken our sense of worth. Inaccurate a gauge as it may be, self-image is greatly affected by our perceptions of how other people see us; other people's acceptance of us affects our view of ourselves.

I think of the inordinate value our society places on beauty, intelligence, and athletic prowess. Few children can meet these strict standards, but they will be accepted or rejected according to their ability to measure up to this distorted and unjust system of worth.

Self-confidence is fundamental to meaningful creative expression. Parents can provide the proper experiences and equipment to elicit creativity, but if our children do not have the confidence to step out and take risks, their creativity will be blocked. How do we parents build in our children the strong egos and indomitable spirits that will sustain them through the inevitable knocks, failures, disappointments, unfavorable comparisons, embarrassments, ridicule, and fears of the tender childhood years? Surely their confidence must be based on a value system more secure than the one which dominates our culture.

Scripture teaches that our worth is grounded in the value the Creator-God bestows on His creatures. We are the apex of God's creation, formed in His very image; we are designed by God according to an individual plan and purpose. Our worth is not based on accomplishment or merit but is derived from God's love.

If children come to a pragmatic understanding of their worth according to *God's* value system, it will profoundly affect their view of themselves. They have an absolute value apart from what they achieve or who they are in comparison to other children. They do not need to look outwardly to an arbitrary standard set by society, but they need to look inwardly to discover God's design for their lives.

Children can then regard their strengths as gifts to be developed and shared rather than a source of pride. "For who makes you different from anyone else? What do you have that you did not receive? And if you did receive it, why do you boast as though you did not?" (1 Cor. 4:7).

Children can then accept their limitations as part of God's design, not as reason for despair.

> But who are you, O man, to talk back to God? "Shall what is formed say to him who formed it, 'Why did you make me like this?'" Does not the potter have the right to make out of the same lump of clay some pottery for noble purposes and some for common use? (Rom. 9:19–21).

The absurdity of anything created resisting the design of its Creator has been captured by Emily Dickinson:

> God made a little gentian—
> It tried—to be a Rose—
> And failed—and all the Summer laughed—

These teachings, however, will be mere theory to children unless the teachings are clearly translated by parents. It is not enough to mouth concepts; they must be demonstrated by parental attitude and action. It is so easy to say that beauty is not important, but what do I actually convey to my children by my response to their appearance or that of others? Day in and day out I can maintain that intelligence or athletic prowess or talent is not all-important, but if my children sense that my approval of them fluctuates according to their report card, team placement, or achievement of any kind, they receive an entirely different message. I must take a hard look at my own values lest I inadvertently transmit a message that betrays my belief.

We cannot deny that our children gain self-confidence both through the recognition of their achievements and through their competence and abilities. However, we do our children no favor if we permit them to base their worth on these fragile, human props which can be all too easily knocked out from under them. We parents can build self-esteem in our children by helping them come to a realistic acceptance of themselves as children who are created and designed by a loving God.

Malcolm Muggeridge tells of being in a chapel at L'Arche, a Swiss community for retarded adults, and overhearing a retarded man pray: "God who made me as I am, help me accept myself as I am." This is not a glib acceptance but is one born of honest self-examination and continual prayer. This acceptance will involve for our children a process of trial and error, of stepping out and taking risks, of testing out paths that lead, perhaps, to dead ends. However, from this process can emerge a healthy confidence that will not only hold them steadily through success but also will sustain them through defeat.

FAILURE

"Ball four! Take your base." The catcher retrieves the ball and throws it back to David who stands on the pitcher's mound. David pitches to the next batter. Even I can see it will be another ball.

Some boys on the front bleacher taunt: "C'mon Rockness, can't you get it over the plate? Why don't they get someone in there that can pitch?"

"Ball two."

"Ball three."

One can sense David's growing tension as the pressure builds. The tighter he becomes, the less control he exhibits; his pitches become wider and wilder with each ball. The coach calls him off the mound.

My heart aches for the dejected figure walking back to the dugout. David has longed to have a turn as pitcher. I know he feels that he has failed his big chance. How I wish I could protect him from the hurt he must be experiencing! I'd like to give those boys a piece of my mind: "What kind of sports are you, anyway? How would you like to be on the pitcher's mound with a row of boys shouting at you?" I'd like to talk to the coach, explain how nervous David was, plead for him to give my son another chance.

As I try to calm my tumult of feelings, I recall an extraordinary commentary of failure I read in *Who's Who in America*, of all places. The entry about Madeline L'Engle, children's writer and recipient of the coveted Newbery Award, concluded with a message from the author:

> Over the years I've worked out a philosophy of failure which I find extraordinarily liberating. If I am not free to fail, I am not free to take risks, and everything in life that's worth doing involves a willingness to take a risk and involves the risk of failure. Each time I start a new book I'm risking failure. Although I have had 25 books published, there are at least 6 fully unpublished books which have failed, but which have been necessary for the book which then gets published. The same thing is true in all human relationships. Unless I'm willing to open myself up to risk and to being hurt, then I'm closing myself off to love and friendship.

144

What would compel a "winner" to write a footnote on failure in a catalog of success? Failure, it seems, teaches lessons that success cannot. All growth requires reaching out, stretching beyond present boundaries to extend one's limits. The checks that come from failure are part of the testing process. Failure forces us to ask tough questions: Where did I go wrong? Could I have done differently? Have I done my best? Through defeat we learn the measure of the challenge; we learn to apportion ambition to ability.

Hardest to bear are self-inflicted failures, those for which we can blame no one but ourselves. Even those experiences instruct us: We mellow through the realization of personal imperfection; we learn toleration and compassion for others who have failed. Dr. Paul Tournier, Swiss physician, writes: "Our successes benefit others, but our failures benefit ourselves."

Who can say we lose when we fail to gain the thing we seek? Failure, by closing one door, opens many others. History is full of failures turned toward good by those who chose to triumph above bitterness and regret. The goal is not to protect children from failure but to help them put it into good use, to make it work *for* them.

Mistakes, misfortune, failure—nothing needs to be wasted. David's disappointment will test the strength of his desire. He may practice pitching to gain the confidence that is acquired only through experience, or he may decide, for now, to be content as catcher—a position he plays very well. The challenge for us as parents is to help our children to accept such experiences as a valuable and necessary part of the learning process; we must teach them in their youth an attitude toward failure that will serve them throughout their lives.

CONFORMITY AND SELF-ACCEPTANCE

"A lady told us if we bring some money to school tomorrow, we can be members of a bird club," explains Kimberly as I tuck her in bed for the night.

"Do you want to join?" I ask.

"Is David joining?"

"I don't know. Does that matter?" I press.

"I'll do whatever David does," she decides.

"But do *you* want to join?" I ask again.

"If David does, I will too," she repeats.

I turn off the lights. A little voice penetrates the darkness: "Mommy, don't forget. Ask David if it is a nickel or a quarter and if he is going to join, OK?"

David, less concerned with the choices of his siblings, is cautiously concerned with those of his peers. He clumps about in thick-soled shoes, formidable impediments to locomotion. He dutifully avoids color-coordinated outfits and opts for combinations that are aesthetically appalling but that are appealing by the standards of his peers. He cheerfully denies his personal preferences when they are found to be in conflict with the mode or manners of his contemporaries.

Through it all I plead and protest: "Do what *you* want. Be an individualist. Don't feel that you must be like everyone else. Think for yourself." Their addictive adherence to convention only convinces me they have emotional needs that must be met through conformity.

A. A. Milne in the poem "Teddy Bear" whimsically captures the relationship between conformity and self-acceptance.

> A bear, however hard he tries,
> Grows tubby without exercise.
> Our Teddy Bear is short and fat
> Which is not to be wondered at;
> He gets what exercise he can
> By falling off the ottoman,
> But generally seems to lack
> The energy to clamber back.

> Now tubbiness is just the thing
> Which gets a fellow wondering;
> And Teddy worried lots about
> The fact that he was rather stout.

Teddy's chubbiness creates within him self-doubt, and in turn he envies those who are thin, until one day he came across

> The picture of a King of France
> (A stoutish man) and, down below,
> These words: "King Louis So and So,
> Nicknamed 'The Handsome!'" There he sat,
> *And (think of it!) the man was fat!*

Teddy, being a thoughtful bear, begins to consider the implications of this picture to *his* plight:

> Why then, a bear (for all his tub)
> Might yet be named "The Handsome Cub!"

The poem is resolved with a happy turn around in Teddy Bear's self-concept:

> Our Teddy Bear is short and fat,
> Which is not to be wondered at.
> But do you think it worries him
> To know that he is far from slim?
> No, just the other way about—
> He's *proud* of being short and stout.

There is for humans, as for Milne's bear, a strange security in sameness. Self-acceptance, it seems, is tied up in the assurance of knowing you are like others, you do not stand alone.

Our children might reach school age so secure in their individuality as to be unconcerned with convention, but it would take incredible strength to maintain that independence through their school years. Dr. H. Paul Gabriel, child psychiatrist at New York University Medical Center, writes of the tremendous pressure put on grade-school children to comply with an accepted norm. "They accord status to classmates, acting as rigidly as the caste system in India and making it almost as hard to move up the social scale. New children are tested and assigned roles. If they are fat or wear 'funny' clothes or stutter or seem uncoordinated, if, in fact, they are different in any way, they become untouchables." How lame must seem a mother's protests against the urgent demands of classmates!

However false or fragile conformity may seem in ideal, it is important in reality. Self-acceptance and social acceptance are related in part to one's ability to conform. Furthermore there is strong evidence that conformity plays a critical role in the learning process.

In 1968, Harvard Project Zero was formed to study the activities of children in an attempt to unravel the mystery of creativity. Throughout twelve years of study, predictable patterns of development were observed. Children passed through an initial stage of encounter with objects and persons of their world before moving on to master the symbols of their culture. It appeared that the "literal stage" which a child enters around seven years of age is the natural and necessary subsequent phase of development. Project co-director, Howard Gardner, commented that

> . . . The common disparagement of the literal stage seems to me misguided. Far from being the enemy of artistic progress, literalism may represent its advance guard. That concern with realism that pervades the literal stage may be a crucial phase of development—the time for mastering rules.
>
> In fact, as youngsters move through the literal stage, most exhibit a gradual improvement in their ability to understand and respond to works created by others.

Could it follow that what appears to be an alarming addiction to convention is in fact a crucial aspect of any learning process? Could Jonathan's imitation of his siblings' behavior or could Kimberly's modeling of David be essential to the development of their own identities? Could it be that as David checks out his contemporaries and matches their performance, he is gaining the social skills and security that will in time free him to experiment with his own self-expression? Could it be that as children acquire the ability to conform to an accepted standard, they will then achieve the confidence to abandon it and rely on their own instincts?

Like it or not, conformity has a valid place in self-development. Our job is not so much to oppose it as it is to help the children master the rules of convention so they will be free to move past them. Although we must continue to urge and support any indication of independent thinking, we must be patient with their need to conform. It is, after all, by conformity to the will and purposes of the Creator that we are led beyond earthly limits to our fullest creative potential.

CAT GOT YOUR TONGUE?

It is the first week of school. I make the early morning transportation rounds.

Kimberly leans forward from the back seat. "I like school better now," she states.

"Why?" I wonder.

"Yesterday I didn't feel those bumps," she replies.

"Bumps?"

"Yes, those *fast* bumps," she says putting her hand over her chest.

"Oh, you mean your heart beating?" I say finally understanding.

"Yes, your heart beating faster and faster when you're shy."

We have all at some time or other felt those "fast bumps," the quickening pulse, the inhibiting constrictions of shyness. Whether it be a momentary impediment, triggered by a threatening situation; whether it be a persistent predisposition toward life; whether it be so slight as to be inconsequential or so violent as to be crippling, shyness is real.

I know the feeling well, yet, surprisingly, it took a "moment of truth" for me to begin to deal effectively with shyness in my children. When David was two years old, we moved one thousand miles away from all things familiar. The friendly little chap who would look people in the eyes and say "Hi," shake hands willingly with acquaintances, and sing his ABC's on cue, withdrew before our very eyes into a well-insulated cocoon. To no avail I would plead, wheedle, and coax: "Say 'Hi' to the nice lady, David. Of course he talks! Tell the lady your name, honey."

One day nearly a year after our move, we were walking to Sunday school; David chattered away merrily. As we turned the corner and came in sight of the church, David looked up and confided, "When we get there, I'm not going to use my words." A sober, deadpan look masked the expressive little face; he took my hand and proceeded in silence.

For one explosive moment the events of the previous months flashed before me in rapid-fire succession, but this time through *his* eyes. I could see from his perch in the grocery cart those massive adults towering over him, those strange faces with strange voices asking, "Cat got your tongue?"

150

Nearby stands mother prodding him on. "Speak, David, speak," she seems to say. Doesn't she know that his throat is dry, and there's a tight feeling inside? There are new people, new places, and always the questions and demands: "Say hello. . . Shake hands. . . Tell them your name . . . Say 'thank you'. . . You know how old you are!" The words just won't come. Mother stands by apologizing, then she moves on, disappointed and displeased.

Bombarded with situations too big to handle, he finds it much easier to tune them out altogether: "I won't use my words," he concludes—no words, no hassle.

That night Dave and I talked for hours. In a time of soul-searching we asked questions we hadn't thought to ask before. What are we demanding of David and why? Have we chosen to cater to adults, whose brief contact with an unresponsive toddler is a forgotten event of a busy day rather than to our child, whose self-image is repeatedly influenced by the mirror of our reaction? Which concerns us more: the "face" he shows to others or his deep inner self? Have we put the "cart before the horse," so to speak, by insisting on his performance when there is still substantial uncertainty within him?

We began to examine our motives for pushing David's performance. Most obvious was our sensitivity to the feelings of well-meaning adults when they are inadvertently rebuffed by our child. Then, too, wasn't it our responsibility to teach him basic social skills? Our own desires, admittedly, further clouded the issue; what kind of parents would stand back and permit such "rudeness" on the part of their child? There is no question about it; a friendly, responsive child makes people feel good and makes parents look good.

As we talked, we discovered that these surface sensitivities were complicated by deeper insecurities. Cultural preoccupation with early socialization has transformed yesterday's virtue (children should be seen and not heard) into today's malfunction. Is shyness a normal response or a serious disorder?

We probed for the source and degree of his shyness. David, we believed, felt good about himself; he was happy when he played at home and was relaxed and spontaneous with his friends. However when he was in new situations, particularly with adults, he exhibited a lack of confidence. Could we by our unwitting action propel his lack of confidence into a more serious lack of self-esteem? Through our demands, which he could not meet, might he begin to question his own worth?

Oh, it seemed so clear discussing our small son over steaming mugs of coffee. What we both desired for David was a healthy personality emerging from a strong character. Yet what conflicts had we created for him by insisting on performance that did not match his inner being? First things first, we decided. First he must develop the sturdy emotional building blocks on which to ground his personality, then he can be all-of-a-piece.

We determined to drop social demands altogether (no more "Sing your ABC's," no more "Say 'hello' to the nice lady") to give him a chance to be himself. We vowed to release him from *our* needs and to concentrate on *his* needs.

At first, when we could, we attempted to shift the focus of attention away from him by redirecting conversation to other subjects. Any effort on his part—looking someone in the eyes, answering a question, saying hello—was considered a forward move and was affirmed as such. The most significant change, however, was in our own attitude; by freeing David (and ourselves) from social pressures, we allowed him to grow and respond in his own time, in his own way.

As we hoped, David slowly began to gain mastery over small, manageable situations that in turn became the foundation for bigger challenges. Through the years we have had to evaluate periodically the delicate balance between allowing for natural development and nudging him toward new challenges. At times we felt certain that firmness was in order. There were times when he was clearly inconsiderate of others and social confidence was not the issue at all.

Frequently Dave and I have been tested in our original resolve. We upheld our conviction that, given time, character would manifest itself in personality. We have continued to support each other in this resolve, and we have not been disappointed. David may never have an outgoing, all-embracing personality, but we know at this point that he is at ease in social situations and confident in his ability to relate to the people in his life.

When we hear David reassure his sister, as he did upon the occasion of "the fast bumps," that "It's OK Kimberly; I used to be shy, too" we cannot help but feel that he has a sensitivity and empathy for people which he could not have developed without his own battle. We are convinced that David's struggle with shyness, like so many human struggles, later served him very well.

ALL BY MYSELF

"Mommy! Look! I got dressed all by myself!" There in the doorway stands Jonathan with a look of pride on his face. Not for a moment would anyone dispute his claim. His shirt is on backwards; his blue jeans are twisted to the side. One sock has a red stripe, the other sock a blue one. Somehow he has managed to roll the shoelaces of his sneakers into two large knots. His hair, wet and plastered to the sides (with the exception of one unruly lock), gives him the appearance of a drunken sailor. I resist the urge to pick him up and hug him; his manly stance forbids it.

How proud he is of himself—and rightly so! It is no little achievement, putting all the pieces on the right places, pulling, zipping, snapping. Watching him casually stand there, hands in his pockets, I am struck once again by the strong relationship between competency and confidence. All the compliments and assurances in the world cannot compare with the deep inner satisfaction that comes from genuine accomplishment.

In our children's early years at home much of their confidence is gained as they master basic living skills. How we applaud when a baby takes hold of the bottle for the first time. Each new advance is noted and acknowledged: drinking from a cup, reaching out for finger foods, manipulating a spoon, then a fork. Eating, walking, talking, dressing—from the earliest attempts to the final mastery of the skill, as children grow in competence, they grow in confidence.

Maxine Hancock writes in *People in Process* that "competency training" is an essential responsibility of parents. She suggests three areas in which children can develop basic competence: personal care skills, helping skills, and survival skills. The importance of this learning, she maintains, is not only in teaching children responsibility but also building in them the confidence that accompanies increasing mastery over their world.

Unfortunately "competency training" is not without problems. Of course I want to see our children increase in self-sufficiency; assistance in household tasks can only relieve my crowded schedule, but what I must go through to get to that point often discourages me from even trying. Children's resistance to work, to say the least, is intimidating.

Kimberly walks by with two pillows slung over her shoulder. "It's hard being in this family," she pouts.

"You think so? You don't think other children have to work?" I test her.

"Well, maybe . . . maybe not. Maybe *their* mothers don't make *them* work."

"Is that good?" I ask hoping she will see her own rationalization.

"It's fun!" she offers.

Teaching a child how to set a table or sort clothing or make a bed is a time-consuming job that strains a parent's patience. It is often difficult to live with the initial results. Do I dare adjust the silver or straighten a pillow when they are finished? What about that lock of hair standing straight up on Jonathan's head? Dare I flatten it before he makes his nursery school appearance? My heart fills with dread when I call for someone to help me with supper and Jonathan answers with a cheery, "I'll help!" No doubt about it, it is easier to do it myself than to go through all that is involved in bringing a child to real competency!

There are, nonetheless, many immediate rewards along that rocky road leading toward self-sufficiency. Children, in spite of their resistance, are not entirely immune to the satisfaction of a task that is well done. Tears and complaints are forgotten when daddy comes to view the week's wash, neatly sorted and folded into appropriate piles on the king-size bed. When we hear the children give their friends an account of their household responsibilities, we realize that they indeed take pride in being useful, contributing members of the family unit. Surely their growing "I can" approach to life might be attributed in part to their growing sense of competence. Confidence gained now from mastering relatively mundane functions becomes the foundation for yet greater creative expression.

Someday, I tell myself, I will make a chart which lists the skills that our children must be taught to prepare them for life. Systematically I will go down the list, checking off each completed item. Until then Dave and I will follow the rule of thumb that has guided us thus far: never do for the children what they can do for themselves. We will continue to expect and tolerate a certain amount of resistance; we will try to overlook the wrinkles in the bedspreads and the untamed cowlick as a fair price toward our ultimate goal: confident, competent, yes *creative* children who contribute in positive ways to their society.

BLUE RIBBON
FOR KIMBERLY

"I lost." Kimberly sets her lunch box on the table and climbs onto the kitchen stool.

"You lost?" I question.

"Yes, I lost," she responds with resignation.

"What did you lose, honey?"

"I lost the art contest," she states in a "what-else-*is*-there-to-lose" tone of voice.

"Did they announce the winners for each grade or just first place?" I probe.

"Each grade. I even checked to be sure they hadn't made a mistake. I asked the lady in charge if she was sure I hadn't won." Her voice breaks.

I glance from my cooking to the little figure perched on a stool, resting her chin in the cup of her hands. How she must have cared in order to work up the courage to challenge the results! I think back on her excitement as she related the details of the city-wide contest. For several days her mind was on little else. She discussed her ideas at great length, sketching out possible designs, then submitting them to the family for comparison. Finally she made the transfer on to "regulation paper," laboring over each detail. Up to the last moment Kimberly could be seen taking out her drawing, scrutinizing it critically, making a careful refinement or two, then going over the slightest suggestion of a smudge with an eraser. Kimberly did her best. Clearly she expected to win.

I look at the child before me. I picture the drawing she entered: the slightly off-kilter tower surrounded with lush foliage, several birds in flight, a squirrel scampering up a tree. Everything in my heart reaches out to her. How I'd like to put a blue ribbon on her drawing and bring a smile to her face. But there are lessons to be learned that are infinitely more valuable than a First Prize ribbon.

Up to this point Kimberly's art has been affirmed and accepted by a completely non-competitive standard. It was something she did well, and that was enough. Now she must come to terms with the added dimension of competition. There is no way to avoid it; outside the home her efforts will be weighed on the scale of comparisons. The recognition of her talents will depend on her ability in comparison to that of others in the same situation. Even when Kimberly has done her best, another may still do better.

This is only the first of many experiences which will put her capabilities to the test. Throughout life she must take stock of her abilities in relation to those of others and proportion her goals accordingly. It is essential to her survival in a competitive world.

At the same time, it is imperative that she not make this artificial gauge the measure of the total value of her gifts or of her worth as a person. The standard that human beings use may be relative, but God judges by an absolute standard: that is, to do one's best. Kimberly must learn not to ask, "Am I best?" but "Am I *doing* my best?"

Winning is wonderful, but it's not of primary importance. Studies reveal and personal experience reinforces that when the only goal is to be in first place, discovery and enjoyment often get lost in the battle. For example, educator Dr. Douglas Heath has found a negative correlation between academic success and happiness in life: "The true test for a successful, enjoyable life was not measured in report cards at all. As it turned out, the gold stars should have been awarded for a person's self-image, his or her inner resources and the ability to handle stress in a positive way." Winning in any area is not necessarily succeeding; true fulfillment rests on something far more essential than attaining first place.

The comparative standard evident in our unquestionably competitive society simply underscores the necessity of working toward one's own satisfaction. There will always be someone "better." Even the "best" are targets for the subjective judgment of their fellow humans. In the final analysis one is more likely to make a significant contribution out of one's uniqueness than from an attempt to achieve an arbitrary standard of success.

Somehow I must help Kimberly to understand this. I must help her to accept that even though her drawing didn't win, *she* didn't lose. The *real* test she has passed with flying colors: she has done her best—a blue ribbon for Kimberly!

A LISTENING HEART

"Mom-*mee!* Don't say 'uh huh.' I don't like you to say that," complains Jonathan in reaction to my monosyllabic response.

"I know," continues Kimberly, "sometimes when you say 'uh huh' you might not be thinking. Isn't that right, mom?"

I look down at the two pairs of eyes challenging me for an answer.

"That's right, isn't it?" insists Kimberly.

"Well, maybe—sometimes" I hedge, feeling properly rebuked.

My children, it seems, are like sensitive instruments, taking constant readings of my every response; they are quick to pick up the slightest indication of my disinterest. Despite the fact that I have developed a fairly sophisticated system of response—varying my inflection and expression, I find it impossible to satisfy them for long with less than my full, undivided attention. Why do my children insist on my complete attention? What does it say to them when I really listen?

Listening says, "What you think and what you say are important. You are important." All the tributes and tokens in the world cannot convey to our children their worth so convincingly or compellingly as the simple and eloquent gesture of listening. Eric Hoffer, a longshoreman-philosopher, recalls the Bavarian peasant woman who cared for him after his mother died:

> And this woman, this Martha, took care of me. She was a big woman, with a small head. And this woman, this Martha, must have really loved me, because those eight years of blindness are in my mind as a happy time. I remember a lot of talk and laughter. I must have talked a great deal, because Martha used to say again and again, "You remember you said this, you remember you said that . . . ?" She remembered everything I said, and all my life I've had the feeling that what I think and what I say are worth remembering. She gave me that.[17]

Transmitting to children a sense of their individual worth would be reason enough to listen, but there are other benefits as well. Children's words give us valuable insights. We discover what they are feeling and

159

thinking; their choice of subjects reveals what is important to them. Frequently problems are sorted out, perspective is attained in the very process of their articulating. Children, encouraged by a genuine interest to express themselves, gain practice in the invaluable skill of transforming thoughts into words.

It's not for lack of knowing better that I give my children mindless murmurs and meaningless nods. I want to listen; I intend to listen, but it seems that so many things—significant or not—clamor for my attention and clutter up my life, crowding out those moments of attention that my family deserves.

The moment which I choose to undertake a task demanding concentration is the very moment David chooses to recount, play by play, an after-school flag football game. Just as Kimberly launches into a recitation of her day at school, the telephone rings; one child's message is preempted by another's skinned knee; all three children talk at once. I rush here and there, delivering children to diverse destinations, running errands, pursuing my plans, aiding in their projects only to discover at the end of a day we have hardly talked at all; we have only nodded in passing. Thornton Wilder poignantly captures this reality in *Our Town* in which Emily relives her twelfth birthday. With the unfolding day comes the increasing awareness of how little time people give to the ones they love. "I can't, I can't go on," she cries. "It goes so fast. We didn't have time to look at each other." Only too understandable, yes, but what are we communicating to each other when we don't have time to listen?

Good intentions, alone, are not enough to secure that precious listening time. We must create the atmosphere and the occasions which facilitate conversation: taking a child on an excursion, extending one child's bedtime past the others, scheduling a "tea party," setting aside a slice of time each day to be accessible for children's conversations. We must capitalize on those natural situations conducive to conversation. We must be alert and aware, keeping our antennae out to pick up the chance moment when a child wishes to talk. Then we must be willing to stop everything to listen. The right time to talk cannot be reconstructed; how we respond at that moment sets the stage for further communication.

Often the times I do spend listening can so easily be tarnished by my lack of sensitivity or understanding. How many times have I cut short a confidence by submitting to the irresistible urge to moralize or instruct?

How often have my efforts to hasten a child's faltering delivery hurried the conversation to an abrupt end? Even my empathy has, at times, interfered with communication as I reached supportive but wrong conclusions rather than wait to hear my child's exact words.

Listening, careful listening, is an art. Like any other art it demands diligent and careful cultivation. It requires discernment to distinguish between chatter and a sincere desire to converse; it takes skill to ask the right questions. We need patience to allow our children the freedom to phrase their ideas in their own time and way. Careful listening requires a sensitivity to know when to terminate if our children do not wish to talk. We need the tolerance to listen without censure or condemnation as well as the wisdom to know when to speak or to remain silent, to challenge or to support. Finally we need the ability to perceive the true meaning behind the words.

Indeed listening is an art. Certainly there are disciplines to develop and skills to achieve if we are to master this art. None of these is so priceless as the natural resources available to each of us: ears that hear and a heart that really cares.

Make mine a listening heart, O Lord. Amid the din and clatter of everyday living, tune my ears to hear, and open my heart to receive my children's spoken and silent messages. Take my understanding, limited and imperfect, and illuminate it with Your insight and Your wisdom. May I turn my children to You, always accessible, ever understanding—the Listener. Thank You Father, for listening to me. Amen.

AND THINGS
THAT GO BUMP
IN THE NIGHT

"Mommy, help me!" Kimberly's scream snaps me back from my daydreaming. My eyes scan the playground until I spot her sitting at the top of the slide. She is paralyzed by a group of barking dogs that have entered the park—dogs of all shapes and sizes. An imposing German shepherd awaits her at the bottom of the slide.

The other children, indifferent to the presence of the animals, shout to her, "Come on, don't just sit there. What are you waiting for? Hurry up!"

Her chagrin finally outstrips her fear; she slides down, races past the dog, and flings herself into my arms.

"I want to go home," she sobs. Her whole body is trembling; tears stream down her face.

"Honey, we can't. We just got here." Firmly I guide her toward the jungle bars, an Airedale hobbling behind us, a cocker circling us making excited, high-pitched yips. Kimberly scrambles like a monkey to the top of the bars.

I return to my bench and watch the children play. They swing and slide, leap from boulder to boulder, skip stones across the water's surface, and dangle from bars suspended over the clear, clean brook. Kimberly, frozen with fear, straddles a bar at the top of the jungle gym while below her harmless dogs romp and frolic.

As I watch her, I review our efforts to help Kimberly overcome her fear. Her father and I have reasoned with her, attempting to help her distinguish between familiar dogs and strangers, calm dogs and "jumping" ones. Faithfully we have pointed out how particular dogs relate to other children. "See how gentle he is with Jonathan. He's just sniffing his hand. He won't bite." Kimberly's initial enthusiasm for the fluff of a puppy we gave her turned to stark terror as he rapidly developed into a muscular mass of energy, forcing us finally to put him up for adoption.

It wasn't that she didn't try. She perched daily on the porch railing, murmuring endearments to Rocky who devotedly sat below with his body quivering from the thumping of his tail. There were other acts of courage—reaching an extended arm to pat the sleeping dog, walking him on a leash. And there were statements of bravado:

"Tomorrow, after school, I'm going to walk all the way to the swingset without anyone holding Rocky."

"Good."

"*Walk*, I don't mean run," she emphasized.

"Good."

"That is, I'm going to *try* to."

Even now she begins and ends her day with the prayer, "Please God, help me not be afraid of dogs."

Despite all of her attempts to handle this fear, despite all of our attempts to help her, she still is afraid of dogs. Glimmerings of encouragement end with setbacks—one step forward, two steps backward. Our efforts to help her face this foe have only increased her fear; we have concluded that we must back off. Advice from Gesell Institute's *Child Behavior* strengthens us in this resolve:

> Withdrawal from a feared object is natural and should be permitted.
>
> The natural period of withdrawal may be long or short, depending on the personality of the child and on how frightened he is. . . .
>
> Tell him that there will be this period of withdrawal and that he can count on your protecting him during the period. This can relieve the tension so that he may be able to resolve his fear more quickly than when he is trying to resolve it alone.[18]

Everything within me shouts for me to insist that she come down to face the foe, to see for herself that she will not be harmed. However our experience has proven that more can be accomplished by communicating our understanding and the assurance of our protection than can be accomplished by force.

We must not add to her fear by forcing her to feel ashamed for being afraid. Kimberly is not the only one who struggles with fear. Jonathan may glibly assure her, "I'm not afraid of dogs, and I'm only three," but much of his daytime energy is expended in fighting the nocturnal visitants of his imagination. He stands with a long rod in his hand (a scepter which has imbued him with power), a swagger, and a deep husky voice.

"I'm big. I'm strong. I'm fast. Watch." He runs top speed to the living room and back to the kitchen. He leans against the stove, head lowered, eyes raised to some far off spot. "There's a monster in the hall. No, not a monster, a *creep*." He raises his rod. "I will go right up to him."

He runs into the hall, manfully flailing his rod at "creeps" who only last night utterly defeated him. Through labored breaths he confides, "I'm big; I'm *David*."

Nor is David "The Big" without fear. He exhibits enormous ingenuity in devising ways to manipulate his younger siblings into being his "courage" in new situations. I am not without fear. The Gaelic Prayer, copied on pretext for the children, is, I confess, as much for me as for them:

> From ghoulies and ghosties
> And long-leggedy beasties,
> And things that go bump in the dark
> Good Lord, deliver me.

Yes, fear is a common human experience. It is, after all, necessary for survival. The problem arises when it becomes crippling or out of proportion to the danger. Yet I must not let myself or others minimize Kimberly's fear just because to grown-ups it seems unreasonable. Real or imagined, secret or known, rational or inexplicable—fear that *feels* real *is* real.

Neither can I indulge her by entirely circumventing the enemy. Dogs are a part of life as are "ghoulies and ghosties and long-leggedy beasties" or whatever may cast their dark shadows over our existence. Nothing would be gained by cutting short our outing in order to cut short her suffering. Who knows what may attract her attention and distract her from her fear?

I do not know how Kimberly will resolve her fear or, for that matter, whether she ever will resolve it. As she grows older, circumstances, no doubt, will give her a different perspective: dogs may seem smaller as she gets taller; she may feel as though she has greater control. She might, through life, walk a wide circle around dogs. But for now, whenever possible, her father and I must be on the sidelines, supporting any evidence of courage and ready with an outstretched hand when needed.

We hope that through our support she will develop the ability to face fear of any "beastie." Should fear remain, I hope she will accept it as normal, understanding that a courageous life is not, in the words of Paul

Tournier, "one exempt from fear, but on the contrary one that is lived in full knowledge of fears of all kinds, one in which we go on in spite of our fear."

Of course we cannot be with Kimberly in every situation. The time will come when we will no longer be near to offer her a hand. I pray that she will have placed her confidence in a Presence far more secure than any human refuge—the One who has "not given us the spirit of fear; but of power, and of love, and of a sound mind" (2 Tim. 1:7 KJV). Then she can say with the Psalmist:

> In you, O Lord, I have taken refuge;
> . . . .
> Into your hands I commit my spirit.
> (Ps. 31:1, 5)

FACING FENCES

"I've made up my mind. Today, I'm going off the high dive—*really*."

Kimberly leaves my side to run to the foot of the ladder. From my desk chair, I see only her hands marking her advancement on the stainless steel ladder: slowly, up—one, two three . . . she stops and backs down. Again she ascends the ladder—one, two three—four! Again she stops and backs down. Oh, the agony! She could be swimming from one corner of the pool to the other; she could be performing cannonballs and can-openers from the pool's edge. Instead she has chosen to submit herself to this singular test.

Since the first day of vacation she has had it in her mind to scale the heights and take the plunge. She has yet to make it past the fourth rung of the ladder. Daily she repeats the questions: "Do you think I should go off the high dive? How quickly do you come up?"

Daily I run the gamut of responses: "Go ahead, Kimberly, try. You can do it," to "Don't worry yourself about it this year; you're only six." My comments have no impact on her whatsoever. The tall, looming presence of the diving board stands as a constant, taunting challenge to her strength.

All morning long she hovers around the base of the high dive. Occasionally she swims with the children, only to return once again to the ladder. Repeatedly she climbs to the third rung, sometimes to the fourth, then she backs down before she reaches a point of no return. I want to shout, "Stop it child. Don't do this to yourself. Don't do it to *me!*" But I can't. She is captive to this challenge. Regardless what I, or anyone might say, for her to end the vacation without taking the plunge would be defeat. It has become, one might say, a mandate of spirit. As much as I would like to stop her—to ease her tension as well as my apprehension —I must let her resolve this for herself.

Children need room to test themselves. It is essential to their development. As they step out in response to a new challenge, they stretch and develop. They learn to tailor their ambition to their ability. To discourage them from new ventures demonstrates doubt in their ability and denies them a chance to test their potentials.

A mother's natural instincts often work against this logic. At birth children are utterly helpless; without protection they would not survive. Still children cannot be insulated indefinitely. In the space of twenty years they must progress from total dependency to full independence. If children are to attain a beneficial degree of independence, they must be given the liberty to respond naturally to the challenges of their expanding world. This is not achieved without risk; dangers are real. Nonetheless since we cannot shield our young from the total gamut of life, we must prepare them for it.

I recall David's early efforts to graduate to a two-wheeled bicycle. Every day he tackled the steely cycle with full understanding of the risks involved. He endured the humiliation and frustration of frequent falls; he suffered the sting of skinned knees and elbows. Repeatedly he wiped back his tears and mounted his bike until one day he proudly sailed around the block without a single fall. What would have been gained by our insisting that he stop? Perhaps he would have avoided a few scrapes and bruises, and maybe he would have been less tense, but bruised knees heal more quickly than spirits crippled by fear. Wounds of both body and spirit were swiftly assauged by the soothing balm of success.

It is not in our children's best interest to overprotect them from any kind of stress. All childhood difficulties—unsympathetic teachers, boring activities, obstreperous playmates, neighborhood squabbles, ridicule, criticism—are but a taste of what our children will experience in their adult years. When they are adults, however, they must face these difficulties on their own. It is infinitely more kind to encourage our children to stretch in order to meet a given problem than to advocate for them or adjust every situation to their advantage. If is far better to help children work through and overcome fears, admit and learn from mistakes, accept or dismiss criticism, tolerate or change unpleasantness, than to attempt to protect them from these realities altogether.

Walter De La Mare says in *Early One Morning:* "In life's long steeple chase the fences have to be faced and our early years are the least likely to be wanting in nerve, agility, and spirit." We need not deny or ignore real danger; we can stand nearby to assist should the task be too big or the risk become too great. But to protect children from the "fences" they face in life is to do them a decided disservice.

My thoughts are interrupted by Kimberly's tug on my arm. "When daddy comes, do you know what I'm going to do? I'm going to ask him to catch me from the high dive. Isn't that a good idea?" With that resolved she jumps into the water to swim in peace during this brief period of reprieve.

When her daddy comes home, he agrees to help her. As he awaits below, she begins her climb. Up, up, up . . . four, five, six, seven, eight . . . without hesitation, she walks out to the end of the board and stops, a fragile figure framed by a backdrop of palm fronds, clouds, and sky. My heart is pounding.

"I'm scared!" calls a trembling voice from the sky.

"I'm here," comes the deep reassuring voice of her daddy below.

She jumps, a wee speck dropping down, down, to the awesome blue depths. Will she never land? Splash! Up she bobs! Sound the trumpets; beat the drums!

She's up the ladder again and off the board. Like a wind-up toy programed to a predetermined course of action, she mechanically repeats the cycle—up the ladder, off the board, across the pool, up the ladder—over and over again. Now she puts a little bounce into her jump. Soon she will be performing cannonballs and can-openers from the heights.

Bravo, Kimberly. Bravo! There may be heights you will not conquer. You may reach the "top" and *not* "jump off." But if you face each of life's challenges with the same grit and determination you've exhibited today, the battle will be half won. Bravo!

THE GOAL

"David, you must come in now and do your chores."

"But, *mom*, I just went out."

"I know, but you have work to do before you can play."

"Can't I play ball for just a little while?"

"You know the understanding. You agreed to do your Saturday chores right after playnap if we let you spend the morning at the 'Y.'"

"I haven't had any *free* time yet, today. I sat around and watched games all morning. As soon as I got home it was lunch time, then I practiced the piano during playnap."

"But, David, that was the decision you made when you chose to spend the morning at the 'Y.'"

"C'mon, mom. Please let me play? I'll do the chores later. Saturday is the only day I can just mess around, and I haven't gotten to play outside at all. *Please*, mom?"

I hesitate for a moment as he argues his case with a certain persuasiveness. Play now, work later—why not? He has been inside all day; Saturday is his only "free day." Why not let him have a little time for himself?

But wait. David made a decision this morning fully aware of the consequences. He pleaded, "Please let me go to the 'Y.' I'll do my chores this afternoon, mom, right after playnap. Promise." In choosing to go to the "Y" this morning he chose *not* to have "free time" this afternoon. Do I release him from the consequences of his choice? What would be gained? What would be *lost?*

Part of the growing-up process is learning to make choices for oneself and accepting the results of those choices. Many decisions we parents must make for our children. The burden is too heavy for their inexperienced shoulders; the risks are too great. We must, however, permit them to make whatever decisions they can since, eventually, they will have to make all decisions.

For Jonathan the choices are small and the consequences are slight.

169

Entrusted with a bag of jelly beans, he can choose to sate his senses with the entire contents or spread the pleasure throughout the day. Within the time frame that outlines his day, he is free to order his play. Kimberly's additional responsibilities and privileges bring additional choices: when to do her homework, how to spend her allowance. Because he is the oldest child, David pioneers new territory for all.

Transferring the choice of decisions to the children, I confess, is not easy for me. I want to make what I consider correct choices for my children. I want to spare them possible dire consequences. I want to make things easier for them when they err in judgment and suffer from their errors. I want to arrange for them to avoid the consequences.

David looks toward me with pleading eyes. Shall I let the boy play while the sun shines and let him work later? What difference will it make? I can remove the frown from his face and restore myself to his good favor. This one instance cannot possibly matter that much.

But what about the *next* time he chafes under his bad choice? Do I ease the pain for him again? Now it is only the choice about how to spend a Saturday. But what will later choices be? Continuing education? A life-mate? A vocation? Can I spare him the consequences of his choices *then?*

When we shield our children from the consequences of their decisions, we merely delay for them the maturation that comes only through making mistakes. As they learn what kinds of decisions yield positive results or negative consequences, they will grow and gain confidence in their ability to make careful and positive choices. This confidence, in turn, leads to a growing sense of competence and self-worth.

The road from childhood to adulthood is rocky and steep. There are ruts and detours along the way. One indication that children are heading toward the desired destination is their increasing ability to make decisions for themselves and to accept the responsibility for their choices.

The goal of parents should be to work themselves out of a job. The attainment of that goal begins with the child's responsibility for simple choices and minor consequences: It begins with jelly beans, homework, allowances, and, yes, the use of free time. It begins *now*.

> A parent is not a person to lean on
> but a person to make leaning unnecessary.
> *Dorothy Canfield Fisher*

LOVED— NO MATTER WHAT!

"I love you," I affirm, handing a cup of water over the crib railing to Jonathan who has called me out of bed at midnight.

"I know," he responds in a matter-of-fact tone of voice. "You love me even when you spank me. And I love you even when I hate you."

I look at the little fellow sitting straight up in bed, sipping slowly from his pewter cup; he is secure in loving us and knowing we love him. In his sleepy declaration I hear this endearing message: I love you and you love me—*no matter what!*"

How important unconditional love is to anyone's sense of worth. What security there is in knowing that, regardless of what I do or say, regardless of my fluctuating fate or favor, *I am loved!*

Unconditional love, without a doubt, is the single greatest gift parents can give their children. Certainly it's as natural as breathing to express love when our children please us with their behavior or achievement, but what about those moments when they are disobedient or annoying, when they disappoint or embarrass us? What do we convey to them then? Children—especially when they misbehave or fail, when they fall short in any way—need to feel that they are loved. Despite their behavior they must know that they are loved—no matter what.

Even now as I regard my child with my heart brimming over with love, I must concede that my love is, at best, laced with pride, ambition, and apprehension; it is tainted by all the imperfections of my human condition. As important as my love may be in shaping the self-concepts of my children, it cannot adequately satisfy all of their needs; my love is both limited and temporal.

God's love, in contrast to parental love, or any human love, is perfect and unending. It alone is the sure foundation on which children should base their worth. All endeavors to build children's self-confidence, important though they may be, are not sufficient. These efforts, like anything grounded in the temporal, are fragile and uncertain. There is no guarantee for ability, position, possession, or any earthly commodity.

171

The only true security we have on earth is the love of God.

We must love our children as perfectly as we can. We must do whatever we can to build within them strong egos and indomitable spirits to face confidently life's challenges. But we must teach them that their ultimate confidence must be in God; that, should all earthly investments fail them, He is sufficient for their deepest needs. We must pray that our children will be enveloped by God's love and sustained by this certainty: "Because *God* loves me, I have worth."

ALL THEY ARE MEANT TO BE

Parents must offer their children moral and spiritual direction in the belief that true creativity is not the result of a free, unbridled spirit but of the creature in right relationship with the Creator.

THE SOURCE

The path opens on to a wide clearing. Before us lies our destination, a small, wooden shelter called The Window-on-the-Pond. Ever so carefully we open the door and tiptoe to chairs lined in rows before a window wall overlooking the water. As the children choose their chairs, I read aloud from the printed sign: "This is nature's show, not ours. There are no scheduled performances. Please be patient."

We sit back and wait for the drama to unfold. In the hush of the little theatre we can hear birdsongs and the deep croaking of frogs. A red-winged blackbird swoops across the "stage" and lights on a feeding station, a wooden stump in the water. Another bird joins him and picks daintily from the seeds.

"Look! There's a cardinal!" whispers David, pointing to the bright red bird strutting back and forth on the narrow beach between the window and the pond.

"See its pointy crown," Jonathan whispers, fascinated by the brilliantly colored cardinal that is oblivious to our presence.

"There's a fish . . . a whole school of fish!" exclaims Kimberly.

Suddenly all three children are on their feet, acutely aware of the water teeming with activity. Water bugs skate across the water's surface.

"Let's sit down," I suggest. "See what else we can see."

Colorful bluejays and red-winged blackbirds make unexpected entrances from various points "offstage." They take the spotlight at the feeding station, then fly out of view. Suddenly, as if on cue, a brilliant wood duck emerges from high reeds and glides smoothly on stage. Another follows closely behind. For once the children are speechless, awed by the splendid ducks that are stunningly marked with red eyes and bright green plummage. They look like brightly painted decoys.

We observe in rivited silence this drama being played out before our eyes: sky, clouds, and trees the backdrop; a pond the stage; all living creatures the cast—a microcosm of nature contained within the frame of a window. Bird, fish, duck: each is content, living out its purpose, being fully what it is meant to be. Cardinal is fully cardinal; minnow, completely minnow; wood duck, wholly wood duck—each follows its own design, governed by an internal blueprint.

Here in this natural setting I can see so clearly the beauty and order that exists when creation lives in harmony with its Creator. And from this picture I catch a glimpse of a bigger truth: each creature reaches its fullest potential when it lives in harmony with its Creator's purpose and design. It would be ludicrous for the cardinal, so exquisite, so perfect in flight, to resist its aerial design and attempt to swim. A cardinal was not designed to swim!

What is true for the animals is essentially true for people as well. The question is not what we intended ourselves to be, but what He intended us to be when He made us. Malcolm Muggeridge asserts, "The true purpose of our existence in this world . . . is, quite simply, to look for God, and, in looking, to find Him, and, having found Him, to love Him, thereby establishing a harmonious relationship with His purposes for His Creation."

Creativity through conformity is a principle beautifully enacted at The Window-on-the-Pond. However the same principle applied to humanity is complicated by this distinction: what the animal does by instinct, we do by our "will." We may choose to conform to our Maker's purposes, or we may choose *not* to conform.

The children are unusually stilled by the scene before them. What do they see? Can they see what I see? It is my challenge to show them that they can reach their fullest potential only when, like the rest of creation, they live in union with their Creator and in harmony with His purposes. I would teach them that true creativity does not emerge from a free, unbridled spirit but from conformity to a loving God who is the very Source of all creativity.

SAVE ME FROM MYSELF!

"Mommy, look! I found a treasure!" Jonathan holds the smooth, glossy shell of a snail in the cup of his hand. "Hey, here's another one!" He bends over from his waist and plucks a shell from between two slats of the wooden pier. "I'm going to find some more." Up and down the pier he paces, keeping a sharp eye for apple-snail shells, hollow containers of limpkins' juicy feasts. His search is rewarded with one more shell.

Ever so gingerly, he aligns his treasures in a straight row beside a wooden piling. He stands back to admire the large and lustrous shells. Then he lies flat, his back against the pier. "You lie down too, mom. It's neat." Side by side we watch vultures soaring overhead, effortlessly gliding on rising currents of warm air, the sun edging the tips of their wings in gold. Boat-tailed grackles call hoarsely to each other across the water, "Check, check, check, check."

"I think I better look at my shells. C'mon, let's go." Jonathan tugs at my hands and pulls me toward his collection; squatting, he picks up each shell, one at a time. He turns each one over and over in the palm of his hand, then he sets it carefully back in position. He selects the smallest shell, a dark one, almost mahogany in color, and stares at it, fascinated.

"Should I step on this one?" he asks.

"I don't think so," I suggest.

"I want to," he concludes.

"If you do, you won't have it anymore," I warn.

"But I want to hear it crunch under my shoe," he persists.

"Don't you want to show your shells to David when he's through with his lesson?" I ask, hoping to convince him.

"I've got two more," was all he said.

For the next half-hour Jonathan repeatedly interrupts his play to walk over to the piling and pick up the same shell. Obsessed by some strange impulse to crush it, he asks each time, "Shall I step on it?" I give him no encouragement.

He gathers up his shells, and we return to the house to meet David. At the porch he makes one final query: "Do you think I should step on this shell?"

"Well, Jonathan, it's your decision; just remember that if you do, you won't have it any more."

"Well, I'm going to," he says with resolve.

"Go ahead then," I say, hoping to call his bluff.

He picks up the dark, round shell that has him mesmerized and deliberately places it on the concrete patio. Hesitating, with one sneaker suspended midair, he flashes me a quick, gleeful grin, then stomps down hard with his full weight. Crackle, crackle, crunch. Act accomplished! Silently he stands over the shattered remains of his treasure, a sober expression set upon his face.

Later, driving home from David's lesson, Jonathan hangs over my shoulder. In the rear-view mirror I can see his face twisting in an effort to gain composure.

"Why did you let me break my shell?" he accuses me.

"Jonathan!" I answer with surprise in my voice.

"My favorite shell is broken," he says full of regret.

"It was *your* decision," I remind him.

He turns to David, "Mommy *told* me to break my shell, and I always do what she tells me. Now, it's broken. That was my favorite shell. It was so handsome inside." He throws himself face down on the back seat, wailing, "You made me break my favorite shell!"

As frustrated as I am with the contrary child carrying on behind me, I would guess my feelings are nothing compared to the frustration he feels toward himself. He, like Pogo, could say, "I have found the enemy, and he is me." I hear in his accusation the plea: "Why didn't you save me from myself?"

Had I realized what his obsession would lead to, I would no doubt have stopped him and spared both of us; it is probably just as well that I didn't. The smashed shell showed him that which all my words could not: the "crunch" was not worth the "cost."

So often Jonathan is the helpless victim of his impulses. "But I *want* to," is adequate grounds for him to carry out his urges.

"I'm going to beat up Paul," he tells me.

"But Jonathan, I thought Paul was your buddy."

"He is, but he said he loves *my* girlfriend so I *have* to beat him up."

Today he lost a "favorite shell" for the momentary pleasure of the sound of crunching underfoot. Tomorrow will he crush a friendship for the immediate satisfaction of a retributive kick in the shins?

The development of self-control is fundamental to the civilizing process. All humans enter the world a bundle of raw instincts, screaming for gratification. It is as we gain mastery over our basic impulses and appetites that we become fit creatures with whom to live. The young boy who gorges all his candy without restraint, who hauls off and slugs another at the slightest provocation, who throws his toys about the room because he is out of sorts with himself, could all too easily become the man who is at the mercy of his selfish desires, who has a string of broken relationships resulting from unbridled aggression, who punishes himself with destructive behavior.

Armand Nicholi II, psychiatrist and professor at Harvard Medical School, notes that the types of problems people bring to a psychiatrist have seen a significant reversal in the past decade. "Previously a great many came because of an inability to express impulses and feelings. Today, the majority come because of an inability to *control* impulses." While it has never been easy to say no to basic instincts, it is even harder today in a culture that places a premium on "self-expression."

Jonathan is such an intense little being, ever bent on living out each impulse. How do we help him develop the self-control to preserve what he considers valuable?

He must be taught he cannot give full rein to every passing urge and impulse; he may hurt someone else or he may hurt himself. He must be restrained when he could harm others or himself. Perhaps the greatest learning will take place when, like today, he lives out his impulses and suffers the results. I pray he will gain from such child-size consequences an understanding of self-control which will protect him from life-long mistakes. I hope that when we are not there to "save him," he will learn to be his own friend and not his own "enemy."

TEACH THY CHILDREN

"A giant has come to fight against God's people. The giant's name is Goliath. All the men of Israel have run away from him. They are afraid to fight him because he is so big, but David is not afraid."[19]

"Mom?" David breaks into the reading. "The Bible is really a Christian history, isn't it?"

"Yes. Who told you that?"

"No one. It just is," he responds.

"Come on!" insists Jonathan who sits with a spoonful of Cheerios suspended midway between cereal bowl and mouth. "Finish the story!"

We proceed with the reading from our Bible storybook, which, like orange juice, has become almost standard fare for breakfast. Through trial and error we have arrived at a simple devotional format that works for us even though the time is frequently challenged and sometimes squeezed out altogether by our busy schedules. We begin by reading a selection from a Bible storybook. The children then pose "Stumper Questions" they have formulated from the reading. Often these questions lead us into discussion; sometimes they are answered with a simple yes or no. We conclude with a brief time of conversational prayer based on two important sources: family members' specific concerns and requests and a photo-wheel which Jonathan zealously carries to the table and rotates to the "prayer family" for that day.

There are variations on this theme: Monday morning follow-up on Sunday school take-home papers, inspirational stories, dramatization of an action-packed biblical narrative. In each of these variations the child-centered principles remain the same: keep it short, keep it relevant, keep it interesting. The children's attention is always the acid test.

Sometimes when I'm rushing about, finding matching socks for Jonathan, tying Kimberly's hair into ponytails, setting out breakfast food, rounding up papers and books for school, I wonder what can be accomplished in a mere ten minutes a day. Is it really worth the effort?

Then I remind myself of the reasons Dave and I resolved to set aside this time daily for family Bible reading and prayer. For parents, today, it is not simply a matter of providing instruction for children but *counteracting* messages that contradict a Christian world view. Through media and classroom our children are daily indoctrinated with a value system and way of thinking that is distinctly secular. Can one or two hours a week at church possibly offset this overwhelming input? Can we afford not to counter what we know they are hearing with what we believe to be true?

Systematic Scripture reading establishes a broad, biblical basis for the values and morals we try to instill in our children. Loyalty, honesty, obedience, and faithfulness become more than words when vividly demonstrated by David, Jonathan, Joshua, Abraham, and Joseph. There is hardly a moral or ethical problem to confront our children which has not been set forth in stories of the Old and New Testaments.

The home provides a nearly ideal learning situation. When the breakfast table is the classroom, the house becomes a laboratory to test teachings and to pursue questions raised by biblical precepts. A regular time of reading and discussion develops an attitude of inquiry that goes far beyond any immediate material and continues throughout the day. A precedent is set for further conversation.

One day while I was washing dishes, Jonathan pulled up a stool and leaned on the counter.

"I like me," he asserted. "I'm supposed to like me."

Intrigued by his perception, I followed up on his comments. "That's right, Jonathan. God made you, and what He makes is good. Of course that doesn't mean that we don't do bad things sometimes."

"That's right," he agreed. "We all are naughty sometimes. David is naughty and you are naughty and daddy is naughty sometimes. Even God and Jesus are naughty."

"Well," I protested, "actually Jesus and God are perfect. That means they are never naughty."

"Oh, yes they are!" he quickly added. "Remember the flood! Now that's what I call naughty!"

Dialogue is encouraged between parent and child whereby natural observations and discoveries can be placed in a God-centered framework. One night as we were walking home from church, Jonathan asked, "How did the moon and stars get up in the sky? Someone got a big ladder and put them in the sky, right?"

"Actually, God put them there."

"That's right. He's the biggest, biggest, biggest in the whole wide world. God doesn't need a ladder."

At other times the questions and discoveries have more profound implications. "It sure is a good thing that dinosaurs are extinct," David said looking up from a library book about dinosaurs.

"You're right; I wouldn't like to meet up with one," I agreed.

"Just suppose," he continued, "now I know this could never be, but just suppose, OK? Just suppose God was extinct. *If* He was, everything would be extinct too, because without God nothing could be, right?"

One can supply facts and information in abundance, but the answers children hear best are the answers to the questions they themselves ask.

Little *can* be accomplished in a mere ten minutes per day, but these ten-minute segments each day of the year throughout the many years of childhood can produce significant results. Through faithful instruction our children can be regularly exposed to the total sweep of Scripture. As they hear of God's dealings with individuals and nations, children will develop a Christian world view and system of values. As they question and discuss these concepts in the context of everyday living, they will be learning to "think biblically."

Our efforts to establish a workable family plan for devotions has forced us to become realistic. There is no material perfectly suited for a five-year differential in ages. Therefore we aim for middle ground, knowing that some material is too simple for David while other material bypasses Jonathan's comprehension altogether. Several mornings each week Dave has breakfast appointments outside the home. Those mornings I assume the lead. We have learned that in this as in other things, if we wait for the ideal moment we won't accomplish anything. The very fact that we have set aside this time at the start of each day, even if it is not always observed, cannot help but transmit to our children the high value we place on the Scriptures and prayer. Our hope is that the precedent which we have established as a family will encourage our children to establish their own personal time for communion with God.

And these words, which I command thee this day, shall be in thine heart: And thou shalt teach thy children and shalt talk of them when thou sittest in thine house, and when thou walkest by the way, and when thou liest down, and when thou risest up.

(Deut. 6:6–7 KJV)

TOO BUSY
TO TRAIN

I sit at the kitchen table arranging the details of my day. This will be a stay-at-home day, a much needed opportunity to tackle long overdue tasks. I list my objectives on a fresh piece of paper, numbering them according to priority: plant rapidly wilting seedlings into clay pots; clean closets overflowing with boxes of unsorted clothing; paste photos, backlogged for over a year, into the family album. Already I feel the heady sense of accomplishment which always accompanies the fixing of goals into writing!

Suddenly I'm aware of covert activity by the corner shelf-rack. Jonathan stands on tiptoes, reaching for a camera which is supposedly safely beyond his reach. He knows he is on dangerous ground. The camera is clearly in the forbidden category of "important equipment"; moreover, Jonathan has been repeatedly instructed not to touch it.

What shall I do? To acknowledge his illegal activity will result in a time-consuming scene; to ignore him will result in license and possible damage. Do I take away the camera, or do I take my chances?

I proceed with my planning.

Crash! My worst fear has been realized! The camera has fallen to the ground; pieces scatter across the floor. Still unwilling to interrupt my schedule to attend to the current crisis, I continue my planning.

"Mommy!" calls a desperate little voice. "Don't look over here!" From the corner of my eye I can see Jonathan furtively fetching the broken pieces and gathering them into his folded arm. He hurries out of the room, calling over his shoulder, "I'll be right back."

He returns to the kitchen and stands at my side. "Promise me you won't go into Kimberly's room, mommy? Please?" Each syllable is saturated with guilt and anxiety.

"Too busy to train," I told myself. "Now is not a good time." But is there ever a good time? Is it ever convenient?

"I don't want to crush my child's spirit with constant demands," I rationalize. "I don't want to create unnecessary conflict." But how many times, like today, do I avoid confrontation because of my own unwillingness to take the time to train?

Training, the kind of training that leads to learning, consumes both time and energy. It begins with a definition of boundaries and the setting of rules. It involves reinforcing good behavior with encouragement and responding to improper behavior with appropriate discipline. It requires following up that discipline with reassurances of love and forgiveness.

One only needs to have seen my young son's troubled face to have recognized the necessity of discipline. There is security when established limits are enforced; there is relief from guilt when wrongdoing is acknowledged and punished. Though the training process may be demanding and draining, the end result is a more peaceful home where family members can function with a minimum of tension.

Rarely in the heat of battle do I consider the long-range values of discipline, but they are no less important due to my shortsightedness. Children's attitudes toward authority, we are told, are shaped during their formative early years; consistent and effective authority within the home becomes a convincing argument for the necessity of authority outside the home.

Furthermore parents' discipline leads to children's self-discipline. Taking the time not only to teach but to *train*—seeing that our children do what they are supposed to do—forms habits of behavior that become the foundation for strong character. Andrew Murray addresses this issue in *How to Raise Your Children for Christ:* "Habits influence the person by giving a certain bent and direction, by making performance of certain acts easy and natural, and thus preparing the way for obedience from principle." Discipline may not guarantee self-discipline, but it makes that goal infinitely easier to achieve!

I study my troubled boy who is burdened by disobedience and duplicity. I cast a longing look at my list of ambitions. What is my choice? *My* plans or *his* peace of mind? Clean closets, potted plants, mounted pictures for *my* benefit or the by-products of training for *his* benefit?

Overdue though it may be, I will add another item to my list and label it #1: The training of Jonathan!

Dear Heavenly Father, help me to have the insight to discipline my children. Forgive me for becoming so absorbed in my plans and projects that I fail to give my children the priority they deserve. May my vision not be so clouded by the particulars of everyday living that I fail to see the bigger picture. Give me wisdom, Father, to provide the kind of training that leads to self-discipline and to a genuine desire to submit to Your loving purposes. Amen.

TO SPANK
OR
NOT TO SPANK

"Hurray! Breakfast cake!" shouts David, hungrily eyeing the thick wedges of buttery coffee cake placed on each child's plate.

"I want juice with my breakfast cake," announces Jonathan as I begin pouring milk into pewter cups.

"Fine, you may have juice but *after* you've finished your milk," I negotiate.

"But juice is good for you," he argues.

"True, but when we have breakfast cake, I want to be sure you've had milk first." I walk around the table continuing to pour milk into cups— first David's, then mine. As I approach Jonathan, he grabs his cup, immediately hiding it behind his back with both hands. Pretending not to notice, I pour milk into an adjacent cup and set it in front of him. Jonathan produces his cup from behind his back and thrusts it in front of me.

"You poured my milk into Kimberly's cup. I want it in *my* cup."

"Jonathan!" I exclaim. "The cups are exactly the same!"

"But this is *Kimberly's* cup!" Jonathan argues. "I want my milk in *my* cup."

"I'm sorry Jonathan but you *must* drink from the cup in front of you."

Kimberly walks into the kitchen and seats herself at the table. Before I know it, she (in total ignorance of the issue) has been persuaded by Jonathan to take for herself the rejected cup and is pouring fresh milk for Jonathan. He takes the cup and begins to sip slowly from it, staring at me from over the rim, waiting to see what I'm going to do about it.

What *am* I to do? I'm tempted to just forget this whole thing and proceed as if I hadn't noticed. It's only a cup, a small matter to make such a fuss about. In all truth, if I had it to do over again, I wouldn't have allowed this to become an issue in the first place. I would have let him keep the cup of his choice and would have been grateful he was drinking his milk!

But I didn't. I said—rightly or wrongly—"You *must* drink from the cup in front of you." And now in defiance he drinks from the other cup.

185

Seeing him watch me with challenging eyes, I realize that *he* knows the issue is more than a cup. The issue is willful disobedience.

What can I do? It is too late for verbal admonition. He understood and he chose, the act is accomplished! Natural consequences would be ideal, of course, but what consequences come from drinking milk? Any logical consequence, at this point, would seem contrived and would only prolong this already protracted ordeal. An old-fashioned spanking, though unpleasant, seems the only option.

The protesting culprit is carried into the master bedroom. Holding him on my lap, I carefully review what he has done wrong and explain why I am going to punish him. Placing him firmly across my lap, I administer three sound spanks to his bottom. I deposit him in his bedroom and assure him of my love; I invite him to return to the table when he is ready.

We eat in stifling silence while Jonathan's distant but accelerating sobs completely drench our already soggy spirits. I ponder in retrospect the age-old question: to spank or not to spank? I consider the objection usually leveled against this favored form of corporal punishment: spankings are too easily and too frequently administered in anger without consideration of other more effective methods of discipline.

Surely it is easy to strike a child in anger. If the goal of discipline is learning, as I believe it is, then other methods of discipline usually are more effective than spanking. Yet there are times with a young child, especially in cases of deliberate defiance, when spanking is an appropriate and effective form of punishment. Short, if not sweet, it settles the case, and it clears the air.

The sobs subside. The children go to their rooms to dress for church; I wash the dishes.

Kimberly returns and tugs on my arm. "There's a little pirate who wants to see you."

In marches Jonathan wearing only underpants and a pirate mask. I kneel in front of him. "I have a little boy who is just your size, but he looks much different from you!"

My son raises the mask, exposing puffy eyes and tear-stained cheeks—and a broad, carefree smile! He throws himself into my arms and gives me a happy hug.

Spanking is something that must go,
Say some psychologists, although
Character building is a feat
Sometimes accomplished through the seat.
Edward Lear

WHAT DO OUR CHILDREN NEED?

"I'm not going to play any more!" Kimberly throws her player to the Uncle Wiggly game on the table and stomps out of the kitchen. She storms through the house to her room and slams the door behind her.

What has come over Kimberly? For the last several weeks she has been impossible to live with. Her peace-making ways have been exchanged for challenge and resistance. Touchy and overly sensitive, she has been quick to read the worst intentions into her brothers' most innocent actions. Increasingly out of kilter within herself, she has become increasingly out of kilter with her world. Why does she act this way? What can be done about it?

I recall another time, not so long ago, when we had a similar problem with David. His penchant for resistance had become insufferable. The simplest request became occasion for rebellion; contact with people brought certain conflict. No amount of appeal or authority could alter his attitude.

Analyzing the situation, his father and I had to admit that our negative responses to his behavior only compounded the problem. We decided to make a concerted effort to convey our love to our seemingly unhappy son and agreed to the following plan:

1. Affirm him whenever possible.
2. Express affection when appropriate.
3. Listen to him without outward indication of impatience.
4. Eliminate unnecessary directives and negatives.
5. Distinguish between "misbehavior" and "childish behavior"; before reacting, ask, "Can this be overlooked?"
6. Rearrange bedtime procedures to allow for a time alone with him for reading aloud.

David's positive response was immediate, radical—even a bit frightening! Does our behavior matter *that* much?

Now then, what about our relationship with Kimberly? I consider for a moment the family dynamics during the past month. Much energy has been expended dealing with Jonathan's behavior; much time has been consumed with David's Little League activity. In all truth, until Kimberly's "personality change," I can vaguely recall her to be only a pleasant and undemanding presence in the home. Is it possible that her very accommodating ways have worked against her? Is it possible we have ignored Kimberly while attending to her brothers' more pressing demands?

Dr. Ross Campbell in *How To Really Love Your Child* speaks of a figurative "emotional tank" in each child which requires love, attention, and security. Whether the "tank" is filled or empty will affect children's behavior. The fuller the tank, the better they feel; the better they feel, the better they act. When a child misbehaves, Dr. Campbell claims, the first question a parent must ask is "What does my child need?" not "What can I do to correct my child's behavior?"

What about Kimberly? What does *she* need? Are her emotional requirements for love, attention, and security being met? Loving her as we do, it is hard to imagine that we could have failed to convey that love to her. But it *is* possible. Caught up in our own busy schedules, we tend to respond only to the children's most obvious demands. Kimberly, generally resourceful and independent, asks for little; it is all too easy to presume on her good nature by giving her little attention. Yes, it is all too possible that we have failed to communicate to her with tangible expressions of our love.

Really when I think of it, communicating love to another is less a matter of time and energy than one of awareness and sensitivity. It's taking advantage of countless, little opportunities to say, "I love you": the quick hug, the friendly touch in passing, a smile, an affirming glance; stopping to look into another's eyes when speaking or listening; taking a few minutes from one's schedule to devote attention exclusively to another.

Through her actions Kimberly has been asking, "What about *me?* Do you still love *me?*"

Through my actions I must answer, "Yes, yes, Kimberly! I love you very much!"

BEYOND BEHAVIOR

"Jonathan took my baseball again!" David accuses with anger in his voice.

"Are you sure?" I question.

"Look!" David points disgustedly to the side of the house.

Sure enough, there in plain view is telltale evidence of crime and criminal. On the ground is a baseball glove and a broom. Under the house is David's ball—just beyond the range of retrieval with the broom.

My heart sinks at the sight of yet another piece of evidence in a growing series of baseball-related crimes. In spite of repeated warnings and threats from his brother, in spite of chidings and punishments from his parents, Jonathan begins his search for the carefully hidden ball immediately after David departs for school. Nothing, it seems, can dissuade him from his dark intent; lure of the forbidden is stronger than respect for law!

David's fury at his younger brother is matched by my growing concern. How do we get Jonathan to *want* to behave? Now we can stand over him with threats and commands, or we can restrain him physically, but what counts is what happens when our backs are turned.

I recall a recent conversation with our young offender: "Jonathan! Don't pick the foam out of your pillow! It will ruin it!"

"But I always do it," he responds casually.

"I know, but you're not *supposed* to," I remind him.

"Well, it's all right if you don't *see* me." Jonathan's idea of morality, I fear, is not getting caught!

David retrieves his ball and continues his complaint. "Mom, make Jonathan stop taking my baseballs. He never returns them. I've lost more balls that way."

"I know, David, but we've tried *everything*, and he still does it. Let me ask you a question. How do you get someone to *want* to behave?"

David probes several possibilities, all the while throwing the ball in the air and catching it in his mitt. "You could punish him," he offers.

"Would that make him want to behave or just not want to get caught?"

"Well . . ." he thinks about it some more.

"What makes you want to do the right things?"

"I want to please you and dad, I guess," he concludes.

"But what about those times when you knew you could get away with something? No one would know. No one would be angry if you did or pleased if you didn't. What made you do the right thing then?"

"I'm not sure—but God would know, and I'd have to live always knowing I'd done wrong." David catches the ball and holds it momentarily in his mitt. "You know, mom," he says thoughtfully, "I think that's the hardest question you've ever asked me."

How do children gain a genuine desire to do what is right? How do they develop a vigorous personal morality? Good behavior, though desirable, is not enough if motivated solely from fear of punishment or desire for approval. How do you get someone to *want* to behave? I must agree with my child, it certainly *is* one of the "hardest questions!"

Bruce Narramore in *An Ounce of Prevention* traces the development of the conscience from birth to maturity. Babies have no set of values or moral guidelines and must therefore be constantly supervised and protected from danger. Towards the end of the first year, infants begin to exhibit initial stirrings of "conscience"; fear of authority and respect of consequences are becoming a deterrent to unacceptable behavior.

In the second or third year children's actions advance from largely external motivations to an internalization of the values and beliefs of their parents. Throughout their childhood years even when their parents are absent, identification with and imitation of their parents' moral code will continue to be a major influence on their developing consciences.

Adolescence ushers in the critical dimension of reexamination. This stage, though frequently marked by resistance or even rebellion, must be considered a giant step forward. As the young adults examine and evaluate the basis for their behavior, they begin to move from an "inherited morality" (observed because they've been *told* it is best) to a "chosen morality" (observed because they believe it is best).

We have a long way to go, I'm afraid, before Jonathan will act from personal conviction in regard to baseballs or any other moral matters! Currently his morality is motivated mainly by the presence of his parents or the certainty of dire consequences. David and Kimberly, I suppose, act largely from fear or respect of consequences and from a strongly "internalized parent." Each phase is important to their development and necessary for maintaining acceptable behavior, but each phase leaves much to be desired. A healthy, vigorous morality must not be based on fear or on a slavish desire to please or on a harsh, condemning conscience but in the firm, inner conviction that this is, indeed, the *best* way to live.

Moral laws, like physical laws, are not random rules agreed upon by a given culture to meet current necessities, but they are universal guidelines designed by a loving Creator for the benefit of His creation. Moral laws are not arbitrary rules inflicted upon a person by parents or church, but they are absolute, written upon the very heart of each individual. C. S. Lewis states in *Mere Christianity*, "Moral rules are directions for running the human machine. Every moral rule is there to prevent a breakdown, or a strain, or a friction in the running of the machine."

I believe this, but if our children are to believe it, they must likewise be convinced of the same thing. Naturally we must establish and enforce these "rules," being careful to distinguish between human standards and God's laws. We must attempt to demonstrate the effectiveness of moral laws throughout our lives. But always we must be ready to give the rationale behind the rules: *why* we work better when we follow the directions; *how* they affect our relationship with others and with God.

It is possible that in the future our children will challenge and test the moral code of Scripture in a serious way. Should that time come, their father and I must accept—even welcome—the challenge as an indication that they are moving beyond mere behavior toward a mature morality.

BROKEN PIECES

"Mommy! Help! I've got a problem!"

I rush to the living room in response to the urgency in Kimberly's voice. "Kimberly!" I shriek, "I can't believe what you've done!" A milky pool of Elmer's glue is spread on the round antique table and is dripping onto the carpet below.

"I couldn't get the glue out of the hole, so I took the lid off. When I squeezed the bottle, the glue all popped out."

"But you *know* you're not supposed to do your artwork in the living room!" I yell. Frantically she attempts to scoop up glue-glutted bits of construction paper.

"For goodness sakes, Kimberly," I continue, "can't you see you're dripping glue all over the carpet? Now you're getting it on my good red chair!" I yank her away from the chair and shove her toward the kitchen. "Wash your hands and bring back some paper towels."

As I gather up sticky bits of paper, a spate of scalding words surge from me: "How *could* you have made such a mess? There's glue *everywhere*. What on earth were you thinking anyway, starting an art project before school? I simply can't believe you!"

There is no response from Kimberly. "What's taking you so long? I *need* the paper towels!" I scream louder. I storm into the kitchen to find a white-faced Kimberly standing frozen in front of the kitchen sink, her hands still dripping with glue.

"Did you hear me? *Wash your hands!*" I enunciate each word crisply.

She doesn't move.

Angered now beyond control, I seize her by the shoulders and paddle her without restraint. "*Now*, wash your hands."

Kimberly wrings her sticky hands; deep sobs rack her slight body. She is totally immobilized. Silenced and shamed by the devastated child before me, I lead her to the faucet, run water over her hands and wipe them dry. With tears streaming down my face, I pick up the weeping child and carry her into the sitting room.

I hold Kimberly in my arms till my tears and her sobs subside. Contrite, I ask her to forgive me and together we pray. Reluctantly I send the tear-stained, puffy-eyed child off to school.

All day I hug my shame close to me. I review the incident over and over again, reproaching myself afresh with each reliving. I try to justify my actions. I was exhausted; we had company non-stop; Dave has been away for over a week; I was up a good part of the night with a sick Jonathan.

The image of a pale, stricken Kimberly blots out my excuses. What have I done to this sensitive child? A knowing look and a firm word is reproof enough for Kimberly. What effect could my searing words and ruthless action have on her? And what about *me?* How could I have lost complete control of myself with such little provocation? I'm heartsick for what I've done to Kimberly; I'm ashamed and disappointed in myself.

And yet I must not forget that Kimberly *was* disobedient in her use of the living room. My unreasonable reaction does not excuse her wrong. Furthermore Kimberly must learn to accept and live with the reality of my imperfection. It is important that she learn early in life not to expect perfection from anyone. Today's incident was swift and clean, I console myself; surely the effect on Kimberly will be minimal.

Still I can't help but wonder about other mistakes I have made, mistakes I know to have affected my young. What about the child whose needs were overlooked too long while I focused on the more obvious problems of another. Or what about the needless power struggle I've created on occasion between myself and a strong-willed child? Is it too late to tighten the reins on a child who's been given too much freedom? Can I compensate for the important training I may have failed to provide my children while I was absorbed in pressing concerns of my own?

And what about those mistakes which I am making now but may not recognize as such until much later—mistakes long in formation, with permanent consequences? Which of my fears and failings will be passed on to my children? What scars of spirit are hidden within their beings as a result of my ill-chosen action or inaction? I think of the mother who stated with anguish: "My daughters are grown and on their own. They have little to do with me or my values. Looking back, I can see my mistakes, but what does one do when it is too late, when the damage is beyond repair?" Even now my children demonstrate attitudes and be-

havior clearly beyond my control. Already I recognize mistakes of my
yesterday in some of my children's problems. And my heart echoes,
"What about my mistakes?"

This story speaks to questions in my heart:

There was a young lad who served in the workshop of a great Italian artist. It
was his duty to sweep the floor and straighten the rooms at the end of the day.
He did his work faithfully and well, requiring little attention from his master.

One day he approached the great artist timidly, "Please, sir, would it be
all right if I saved for myself the bits of broken glass you throw on the floor?"

"Do as you please—they are of no use to me."

Days grew into years. The lad faithfully carried out his tasks. Daily he
sifted through the discarded bits of glass. Some he would set aside, others he
would throw out.

One day the master entered a little used storeroom and quite by chance
came across a carefully hidden piece of work. Bringing it to the light, he was
dazzled by the brilliance of a noble work of art. "What is the meaning of
this?" he wondered aloud. He called his servant to him. "What great artist
has hidden his masterpiece here?"

"Master," responded the astonished young man, "it is just my poor work.
Don't you remember—you said I could have for myself the glass you threw to
the floor. These are but the broken pieces."[20]

God, I believe, is the great redeemer of all circumstances. There is no
situation resulting from either sin or ignorance that is beyond His recon-
struction. While neither I—nor sometimes others—can escape the consequences of my actions, when I turn to Him with a humble heart and put
at His feet, so to speak, the shattered segments of my life, He will take
those broken pieces and make from them something good.

We cannot deny the existence of brokenness nor the corresponding
pain and hurt, yet there is nothing to be gained in staring at the broken
pieces. Once we have, in true repentance, turned from our error, making
every possible reparation, we must gather the remaining pieces and give
them once and for all to the One who has promised to work all things for
the good of those who love Him. The final design may not be what it
would have been; the individual parts may be imperfect, yet the Great
Redeemer can take *all* the pieces and make from them a work of art
excelling our human imaginings.

I think of the facsimile of the famed rose window of Notre Dame, reproduced on a disk of leaded glass, suspended in our kitchen window. The sun shining through the glass creates a lyrical play of colors. Deep blues, greens, reds, and yellows are illuminated with varying intensity in the changing light of day. This catch of joy lifts my spirit when the fine glow of colors unexpectedly captures my attention during daily chores. But beyond that, it holds for me a significance far greater than an aesthetic appeal. It is a daily reminder of an important truth: God is the redeemer of all circumstances. When I wreak havoc with a situation, as I did today with Kimberly, its glowing presence radiates this message: go now and make things right where you can, then release the broken pieces to the workmanship of the Master Craftsman. When I am tormented by past mistakes and anxious for the future, it illumines the dark recesses of my soul with this ray of hope: "In all things God works for the good of those who love him" (Rom. 8:28).

Just as certainly as I have made mistakes in the past, I will make mistakes in the future. Such is the inevitable reality of my broken human condition. I can choose to finger the fractured fragments of my life, scrutinizing them with self-reproach, or I can release them to God and view instead the emerging masterpiece being crafted from those same fragments by the skillful hands of the Master Artist.

THE WAY

"My, how your children have grown! . . . You don't mean this is the *baby*? . . . They certainly are growing up!" So comment the old-timers who, like us, migrate yearly to this oceanside retreat in Key Biscayne.

"I remember the first time I saw you," a Cuban waiter recalls in broken English. "You had one there (pointing to my stomach) and one here (making a mock cradle of his arms) and one down there (marking the height of a toddler with the outstretched palm of his hand)!"

Another year has come and gone, and like every other one it has left unmistakable traces of the passage of time. Yet this year more than the others has brought an accelerated sense of the transience of time: David's broadening shoulders and thickening muscles are an all-too-obvious reminder that he is approaching adolescence; Kimberly, leggy and lanky, has lost her little-girl roundness; and Jonathan, wee Jonathan, cannot by the farthest stretch of the imagination be considered a toddler.

"And the seasons, they go round and round, and the painted ponies they go up and down; we're captives on a carousel of time," sings popular singer Joni Mitchell. Round and round we spin, faster and faster it seems. How I'd like to dismount for a moment or slacken the speed for a season, but the carousel continues its relentless rotation. And with each revolution we advance closer to the time the children will leave home. Will they be ready? Are we giving them what they need? Will they "turn out" all right?

Risky business, being a parent! Uncertainty and conflict are constant companions. The beginning is a floundering sensation of being in water over my head. I who struggle to govern even myself, must also govern three young children. What have I to recommend myself? A few years' head start and a small suitcase of experience. I face, as well, that constant dilemma of whether to "assert parental authority" or "permit child autonomy." At what point does the one stop and the other begin?

Where are the answers? Where are the assurances? We look to those

197

who've traveled the road before us. Some offer a point of view and make suggestions. An equal number just shake their heads. "Things aren't like they used to be," they commiserate. "I'm glad my children are grown." They've forgotten, I console myself, but statistics of domestic disaster support their case.

There's an endless array of "how-to's" for child rearing. "Three easy steps to cure tantrums," reads well in print but applied to our raging youngster, they seem glib and facile. "Feeding problems," "Independence," "Lying," "Shyness," "Sibling Rivalry" are attractive titles in an index, but, as antidotes for our children's problems, they seldom are sufficient. The Scripture is strong in principles, but I have yet to find within those holy pages a cure for bedwetting! There is recourse in prayer, but, oh, what I'd give for handwriting on the wall!

However helpful these human and divine resources may be, there are elements inherent to this vocation which make parents pioneers without precedent or pattern. We work with unknown quantities. Each child is unique. Change, flux, growth are programed into their natures. No sooner have we deciphered the code to our children's personalities than they confound us with complications or change. Furthermore the future remains a mystery. We can plot a journey based on present information, but an unexpected twist here or turn there can alter the route altogether. How can we, to whom our children remain enigmas, know what's best for them? How can we, to whom the future is unknown, chart their course with accuracy?

Moreover there is heartbreaking evidence that parents can give wisely and devotedly to their children, who may, in turn, deny the values they have been taught and reject the very parents who love them. It would seem it is not so simple as cause and effect, that no family is immune from failure. The stakes are high; the returns can be low.

What then must we conclude? Are our attempts to build confidence and character in our children only a charade? Are our endeavors to lead them toward creative living merely a complex game of chance? If so, why bother? Why squander our precious time and energy on lives over which we have no control? Let the children go their way, and we'll go ours. Why not?

At times abdication has appeal, but we do not have that choice. It is not even an option. Our children, according to Scripture, are God-given trusts. However inexperienced or ineffective we may feel, however inadequate or inept we may be, by virtue of giving them birth we must also give them guidance and direction. Despite all the uncertainties of raising children, our role is certain: to train, to guide, to instruct. We are not, however, accountable for their response. They have wills of their own; they are accountable for their actions. Our concern is investment, not returns.

True parenthood belongs to God. To Him alone are we accountable. Parents are accountable for the investment in our living trusts; children are accountable for their responses to that investment. The parenthood of God not only liberates us from accountability for our children's actions, but strengthens us in our roles as parents. The heavenly Father, not bound as we are by human limitations, has full knowledge of our children and complete knowledge of the future. It is His intention that we earthly parents benefit from His knowledge: "Trust in the Lord with all your heart and lean not on your own understanding; in all your ways acknowledge him, and he will make your paths straight" (Prov. 3:5–6).

God states clearly in Scripture His desire to be in relationship with His creation and has gone to inconceivable lengths to secure that end. Malcolm Muggeridge writes: ". . . God leaned down to become a Man . . . in order that men might reach up and relate themselves to Him, their Creator." Repeatedly God promises His presence and His power to anyone joined to Him through belief in Christ.

Herein is our ultimate hope and our only real security: *that in union with their Creator our children will reach their fullest potential*. Without minimizing the importance of parental input, I would go so far as to say that all our efforts to provide for our children proper environment, equipment, exposure, to build in them confidence and character are secondary to their establishing a relationship with the Creator. It is only logical that the One who created our children, who knows their hidden talents and potentialities, who knows the unpredictable twists and turns of the future, and who has promised to give guidance and direction would lead them into the richest and fullest living possible. God, I am convinced, is the direct route to *true* creativity; He *is* Creativity.

How I wish we could be certain that our children would commit their lives into God's care; how I wish we could be certain they would seek His guidance in their daily walk. We cannot. They, like us, are free to choose. But of this we can be sure: God loves them more fully and perfectly than we do; He wants them for His own and reaches out to them. If their heavenly Father feels the freedom of choice is worth the risk of rejection, we too, must rest in that judgment.

I cannot help but believe our efforts will make a difference in their lives. Surely it will be easier for them to make sound decisions from emotional building blocks formed of love, discipline, and nurture rather than from the shifting sands of neglect. And no matter what the outcome, we can still rest assured that we have tried to give our best, however limited or imperfect it might have been.

Thus in spite of the reality of risk, fear of failure, lack of guarantees, we must continue to chart an uncertain course through unknown territory. I will pray, I will pray daily, that in our efforts to guide them we will not lose sight of the ultimate goal—to lead our children into loving relationship with their heavenly Father, the Creator-God.

EPILOGUE

Kimberly gives me her yellow paper-bound "Book of Poems." She writes of sunshine, colors, nighttime, flowers, and herself. One line, in particular, stands out: "God made me. He made me in a very special way. No one else is made my way." With the direct simplicity of a child, she captures the essence of individuality. The Cistercian monk, Thomas Merton, elaborates on this subject in his book *Seeds of Contemplation*.

> No two created beings are exactly alike. And their individuality is no imperfection. On the contrary: the perfection of each created thing is not merely in its conformity to an abstract type but in its own individual identity with itself. . . .
>
> Therefore, each particular being, in its individuality, its concrete nature and entity, with all its own characteristics and its private qualities and its own inviolable identity, gives glory to God by being precisely what He wants it to be here and now, in the circumstances ordained for it by His Love and His infinite Art.

What parents have held a newborn babe in their arms without feeling an overwhelming sense of awe, keenly aware that this infant has been "fearfully and wonderfully made" (Ps. 139:14)? Implicit in this tiny, newly-formed bundle of life is promise, possibility, potentiality. Each development is a gain. Each gain suggests yet greater promise, possibility, potentiality. A baby sways to the beat of a tune. Will he be a musician? With amazing dexterity a toddler constructs a complex pyramid of blocks. Will she be an engineer? The young grade-schooler pitches a ball with a strong right arm. Watch out major leagues! Newly acquired skills fan new hopes. A poem, a painting, or an invention evokes a future poet, artist, or scientist.

How easy it is to read into our children our own hopes and dreams, to translate each evidence of talent into concrete future terms. How tempting it is to push our children into our *own* plan for their lives.

We must not. God alone possesses the secret of identity. To each

201

person, individually, will He reveal that plan. Only God can make a child become the person he or she was meant to be.

I offer a charge to my children and to myself:

> To my children—
>> Do not conform any longer to the pattern of this world,
>>> but be *transformed* by the renewing
>> of your mind. Then you will be able to test and approve
>>> what God's will is—his good, pleasing and
>>> perfect will.
>
> *(Rom. 12:2)*

> To myself—
>> Let each become all that
>> He was created able of being
>> Expand, if possible, to his full growth
>> And show himself at length
>> In his own shape and stature
>> Be these what they may.
>
>> *Carlyle*

NOTES

[1]Walter De La Mare, *Early One Morning* (New York: Octagon Books, 1977), 147.

[2]Ibid., 5.

[3]Gabriel Setoun, "How the Flowers Grow," *My Poetry Book: An Anthology of Modern Verse for Boys and Girls*, Grace T. Hufford et al., eds. (New York: Holt, Rinehart & Winston, Inc., 1956), 245.

[4]Rudolf Dreikurs and Vicki Soltz, *Children: The Challenge* (New York: Hawthorn Books, Inc., 1964), 116.

[5]James Dobson, "Table Scraps," *Eternity* (May 1978): 24.

[6]Ibid.

[7]Plato as paraphrased by Abram Chasins, "The Hidden Talents for Music in Every Child," *McCall's* (July 1964): 133.

[8]Brewster Ghiselin, ed., *The Creative Process* (New York: W. W. Norton & Co., Inc., 1952), 25.

[9]Phyllis Theroux, "How to Find the Joy of Being Yourself," *House & Garden* (February 1978): 104.

[10]Gladys Hunt, *Ms Means Myself* (Grand Rapids: Zondervan Publishing House, 1972), 60.

[11]Mary Ellen Chase, "Recipe for a Magic Childhood," *Ladies Home Journal* (book edition) (May 1951): 20, 27.

[12]Jacob Bronowski, "How to Encourage Your Natural Creativity," *House & Garden* (November 1977), 218.

[13]Joyce Hifler, *To Everything a Season* (New York: Doubleday & Co., 1969), 89.

[14]Rachel L. Carson, *The Sense of Wonder* (New York: Harper & Row Publishers, Inc., 1956), 42–43.

[15]Ibid., 45.

[16]John Ruskin, *Sesame & Lilies* (New York: E. P. Dutton, 1953), 60.

[17]Calvin Tomkins, *Eric Hoffer: An American Odyssey* (New York: E. P. Dutton, 1968), 9–10.

[18]Frances L. Ilg and Louise Bates Ames, *Child Behavior* (New York: Harper & Row Publishers, Inc., 1955), 164.

[19]Kenneth Taylor, *The Bible in Pictures for Little Eyes* (Chicago: Moody Press, 1956).

[20]Retold from Mrs. Charles E. Cowman, *Mountain Trailways for Youth* (Grand Rapids: Zondervan Publishing House, 1947), 126.

RECOMMENDED READING

Barzun, Jacques, *Teacher in America*, New York: Doubleday & Co. Inc., 1945.

Written by an educator for educators. A challenging book with relevance to parents for gaining an understanding of the nature and goals of education.

Bettelheim, Bruno, *The Uses of Enchantment*, New York: Random House, Inc., 1975.

A child psychologist's brilliant and moving revelation of the enormous and irreplaceable value of fairy tales—how they educate, support, and liberate the emotions of children.

Boston Children's Medical Center, *What To Do When There's Nothing To Do*, New York: Delacorte Press, 1967.

Practical ideas from a pediatric medical staff for mothers who don't know what to do when their children "don't know what to do!"

Campbell, D. Ross, *How To Really Love Your Child*, Wheaton: Victor Books, 1977.

Important insight from a child psychologist into temperament types and emotional needs of children.

Carson, Rachel, *The Sense of Wonder*, New York: Harper & Row, Publishers, 1956.

Words and pictures to help adults keep alive children's inborn sense of wonder and renew one's own delight in the mysteries of earth, sea, and sky.

Chase, Mary Ellen, *Recipe for a Magic Childhood*, Philadelphia: The Curtis Publishing Co., 1951.

Delightful first-hand account of acquiring in the home the love of and respect for good books.

de la Mare, Walter, *Early One Morning*, New York: MacMillan, 1935, re-
    printed by Octogon Books, 1977.

> Rare insight into children and childhood through a study of early
> memories and writings from many "witnesses."

Dobson, James, *Hide or Seek*, Old Tappan: Fleming H. Revell Company, 1974.

> Presents ten comprehensive strategies by which parents can cultivate
> self-esteem in a child.

Dobson, James, *The Strong-Willed Child*, Wheaton: Tyndale House Publishers,
    1978.

> Guidance in shaping the will of a child without breaking his spirit.

Dreikurs, Rudolf, *Children: The Challenge*, New York: Hawthorne, 1964.

> Practical application of strong methods for child-rearing. Employs natural
> and logical consequences in dealing with misbehavior.

Erikson, Erik, *Childhood and Society*, New York: W. W. Norton, 1950.

> This study of childhood is recommended chiefly for a strong rationale for
> "play" developed in the chapter "Toys and Reasons" (pp. 209–41).

Ginott, Haim, *Between Parent and Child*, New York: MacMillan, 1965.

> Offers strong practical suggestions for effective communication with chil-
> dren, but must be read discerningly since he leans toward a permissive
> view of discipline.

Gheslin, Brewster, *The Creative Process*, Berkeley: The Regents of the Univer-
    sity of California, 1952.

> Thirty-six highly creative people describe their work. In a provocative
> introduction to these essays, the editor draws, from their contributions,
> perceptive and practical observations about the creative process.

Hainstock, Elizabeth, *Teaching Montessori in the Home*, New York: Random
    House, 1968.

> Application of Montessori methods of teaching the young child in the
> home environment.

Hancock, Maxine, *People in Process*, Old Tappan, New Jersey: Fleming H. Revell, 1978.

Writing from her own experience of raising four children, the author shows how parents can help develop confidence, character, and creativity in children during the crucial pre-school years.

Hunt, Gladys, *Honey for a Child's Heart*, Grand Rapids: Zondervan Publishing House, 1969.

A parent's guide to the imaginative use of books in the home. Contains an invaluable bibliography of children's literature.

Ilg, Francis and Ames, Louise, *The Gesell Institute's Child Behavior*, New York: Harper & Brothers, 1955.

Practical advice regarding specific problems and anxieties which commonly arise in child-rearing. Contains an excellent section presenting predictable "Ages and Stages" from birth to ten years of age. A sensitive, straightforward approach derived from extraordinary clinical contact with children from infancy to adolescence.

May, Rollo, *The Courage To Create*, New York: W. W. Norton, 1975.

Explores the nature of creativity—and how the release of this power makes life richer and more satisfying.

Murray, Andrew, *How To Raise Your Children for Christ*, Minneapolis: Bethany Fellowship, Inc., 1975.

Fifty-two devotional readings based on biblical principles for child-rearing. This new edition of an out-of-print volume is as relevant today as it was when first printed decades ago.

Narramore, Bruce, *An Ounce of Prevention*, Grand Rapids: The Zondervan Corporation, 1973.

A parent's guide to the moral and spiritual growth of children. A particularly helpful explanation of the development of a conscience—birth through adolescence—to a "mature morality."

Narramore, Bruce, *Help! I'm a Parent*, Grand Rapids: The Zondervan Corporation, 1972.

Presents basic methods of discipline and helps parents determine the most effective method for specific situations. An excellent standard "text" for child-rearing.

O'Connor, Elizabeth, *The Eighth Day of Creation*, Waco, Texas: Word Books, 1971.

On gifts and creativity. Includes exercises to aid in the discovery and development of one's own innate gifts. Each section is supplemented with writings from a broad spectrum of creative people.

Piaget, Jean.

The Swiss psychologist's first-hand studies have richly contributed to an understanding of the process by which children build a basic framework of thought. Books by Piaget or about his methods give invaluable insight into how children learn. *Piaget Sampler,* edited by Sarah F. Campbell (New York: John Wiley & Sons, Inc., 1976) is unique in being the first anthology to introduce readers to Piaget's theories and experiments through his own writings.

Schaeffer, Edith, *Hidden Art*, Wheaton: Tyndale House Publishers, 1971.

Explores the creative possibilities to be discovered and nurtured within the context of everyday living for parents and children.

Schaeffer, Edith, *What Is a Family?* Old Tappen: Revell Company, 1974.

Examines the role of the family as the "birthplace for creativity" along with other vital functions.

Taylor, Kenneth, *The Bible in Pictures for Little Eyes*, Chicago: Moody Press, 1956.

A Bible storybook for pre-school children. Chronological overview of Scripture. A short paragraph, attractive picture, and simple discussion questions for each selection.

Tournier, Paul, *The Adventure of Living*, Harper & Row, Publishers, 1965.

A challenging philosophy of living, encouraging the reader to make commitments and take risks requisite to reaching one's full potential.

Voss, Catherine, *The Child's Story Book*, Grand Rapids: Wm. B. Eerdman's Publishing Co., 1949.

The Bible in story form, from Genesis to Revelation. A remarkably strong retelling of Scripture for grade school children with fidelity to biblical text and in picturesque style.

Wilt, Joy, *Happily Ever After*, Waco: Word Incorporated, 1977.

Offers practical hints for meeting children's emotional, spiritual, creative, and intellectual needs. A special section dealing with "death, divorce and other 'sticky subjects.'"